FREEDOM
OF THE
PRESS 2004

FREEDOM OF THE PRESS 2004

A Global Survey of Media Independence

Edited by Karin Deutsch Karlekar

WITH ESSAYS BY
BRIAN KATULIS,
JEREMY DRUKER AND DEAN COX,
AND RONALD KOVEN

FREEDOM HOUSE
NEW YORK ▪ WASHINGTON, D.C.

ROWMAN & LITTLEFIELD PUBLISHERS, INC.
LANHAM ▪ BOULDER ▪ NEW YORK ▪ TORONTO ▪ OXFORD

ROWMAN & LITTLEFIELD PUBLISHERS, INC.

Published in the United States of America
by Rowman & Littlefield Publishers, Inc.
A wholly owned subsidiary of The Rowman & Littlefield Publishing Group, Inc.
4501 Forbes Boulevard, Suite 200, Lanham, MD 20706
www.rowmanlittlefield.com

P.O. Box 317, Oxford OX2 9RU, United Kingdom

ISSN 1551-9163
ISBN 0-7425-3648-3 (cloth : alk. paper)
ISBN 0-7425-3649-1 (pbk. : alk. paper)

Printed in the United States of America

♾™ The paper used in this publication meets the minimum requirements of
American National Standard for Information Sciences—Permanence of Paper for
Printed Library Materials, ANSI/NISO Z39.48-1992.

Table of Contents

Acknowledgments

Freedom of the Press 2004 could not have been completed without the contributions of numerous Freedom House staff and consultants. Freedom House would like to thank the World Press Freedom Committee, the Freedom Forum, and Bette Bao Lord for their generous contributions toward our ongoing work to promote freedom of expression. Additional support for this year's survey was provided by The Lynde and Harry Bradley Foundation, the Lilly Endowment, and the F. M. Kirby Foundation.

This year's survey was written by Karin Deutsch Karlekar, Mark Rosenberg, Jane Stockman, Sarah Repucci, Leigh Tomppert, Aili Piano, Michael Goldfarb, Arch Puddington, Yves Sorokobi, Brian Katulis, Ana Andjelic, Paula Schriefer, Jennifer Whatley, Felicity Amos, Joseph McSpedon, Ignacio Prado, Vanessa Brown, and Ryan Gottschall. Freedom House would also like to thank Ronald Koven, European representative of the World Press Freedom Committee, Jeremy Druker and Dean Cox, and Brian Katulis, for their contributions.

We are grateful for the insights provided by those who served on this year's review team, including Freedom House staff members Jennifer Windsor, Arch Puddington, Christopher Walker, Leonard R. Sussman, and Adrian Karatnycky, as well as Mark Bench and Ronald Koven of the World Press Freedom Committee and Ann Olson of the International Center for Journalists. In addition, the ratings and narratives were reviewed by a number of regional and country analysts, including Charles Graybow

(Asia), Martin Edwin Andersen (Latin America), Yves Sorokobi (Africa), Brian Katulis (Middle East and North Africa), and Amanda Schnetzer, Aili Piano, Margarita Assenova, Stuart Kahn, Mike Stone, John Kubiniec, Mike Staresinic, Cristina Guseth, and Roland Kovats (Central and Eastern Europe and the Former Soviet Union). This report also reflects the findings of the Freedom House study *Freedom in the World 2004: The Annual Survey of Political Rights and Civil Liberties.*

Karin Deutsch Karlekar, a senior researcher at Freedom House, served as managing editor of this year's survey. Overall guidance for the project was provided by Arch Puddington, director of research, and by Christopher Walker, director of studies. Research, editorial, and administrative assistance was provided by Sarah Repucci, Mark Rosenberg, Jane Stockman, Amy Phillips, and Elizabeth Howell. Anne Green, of Greenways Graphic Design, was responsible for the design and layout of the book, while Nancy van Itallie served as the principal copy editor.

Survey Methodology

This survey of 192 countries and one territory expands a process conducted since 1980 by Freedom House. The findings are widely used by governments, academics, and the news media in many countries. The degree to which each country permits the free flow of information determines the classification of its media as "Free," "Partly Free," or "Not Free." Countries scoring 0 to 30 are regarded as having "Free" media; 31 to 60, "Partly Free" media; and 61 to 100, "Not Free" media. The criteria for such judgments and the arithmetic scheme for displaying the judgments are described below. Assigning numerical points allows for comparative analysis among the countries surveyed as well as facilitating an examination of trends over time.

Criteria

This study is based on universal criteria. The starting point is the smallest, most universal unit of concern: the individual. We recognize cultural differences, diverse national interests, and varying levels of economic development. Yet Article 19 of the Universal Declaration of Human Rights holds that:

> Everyone has the right to freedom of opinion and expression; this right includes freedom to hold opinions without interference and to seek, receive, and impart information and ideas through any media regardless of frontiers.

The operative word for this survey is *everyone*. All states, from the most democratic to the most authoritarian, are committed to this doctrine through the UN system. To deny that doctrine is to deny the universality of information freedom—a basic human right. We recognize that cultural distinctions or economic underdevelopment may limit the volume of news flows within a country, but these and other arguments are not acceptable explanations for outright centralized control of the content of news and information. Some poor countries allow for the exchange of diverse views, while some developed countries restrict content diversity. We seek to recognize press freedom wherever it exists, in poor and rich countries, as well as in countries of various ethnic, religious, and cultural backgrounds.

This survey does not assess the degree to which the press in any country serves responsibly, reflecting a high ethical standard. The issue of "press responsibility" is often raised to defend governmental control of the press. Indeed, a truly irresponsible press does a disservice to its public and diminishes its own credibility. However, governmental efforts to rein in the press on the pretext of making the press "responsible" has far worse results, in most cases. This issue is reflected in the degree of freedom in the flow of information as assessed in the survey.

Sources

Our data come from correspondents overseas, staff travel, international visitors, the findings of human rights and press-freedom organizations, specialists in geographic and geopolitical areas, the reports of governments and multilateral bodies, and a variety of domestic and international news media. We would particularly like to thank other members of the International Freedom of Expression Exchange (IFEX) network for providing detailed and timely analyses of press freedom violations in a variety of countries worldwide.

Methodology

Through the years, we have refined and expanded our methodology. Recent changes to our methodology are intended to simplify the presentation of information without altering the comparability of data for a given country over the 24-year span, or of the comparative ratings of all countries over that period.

Our examination of the level of press freedom in each country is divided into three broad categories: the legal environment, the political environment, and the economic environment.

▌ The **legal environment** encompasses an examination of both the laws and regulations that could influence media content and the government's inclination to use these laws and legal institutions in order to restrict the media's ability to operate. We assess the positive impact of legal and constitutional guarantees for freedom of expression; the potentially negative aspects of security legislation, the penal code and other criminal statutes; penalties for libel and defamation; the existence of and ability to use freedom of information legislation; the independence of the judiciary and of official media regulatory bodies; registration requirements for both media outlets and journalists; and the ability of journalists' groups to operate freely.

▌ Under the category of **political environment,** we evaluate the degree of political control over the content of news media. Issues examined in this category include the editorial independence of both the state-owned and privately-owned media; access to information and sources; official censorship and self-censorship; the vibrancy of the media; the ability of both foreign and local reporters to cover the news freely and without harassment; and the intimidation of journalists by the state or other actors, including arbitrary detention and imprisonment, violent assaults, and other threats.

▌ Our third category examines the **economic environment** for the media. This includes the structure of media ownership; transparency and concentration of ownership; the costs of establishing media as well as of production and distribution; the selective withholding of advertising or subsidies by the state or other actors; the impact of corruption and bribery on content; and the extent to which the economic situation in a country impacts the development of the media.

Ratings

Each country is rated in these three categories, with the higher numbers indicating less freedom. A country's total score is based on the total of the three categories: a score of 0–30 places the country in the Free press group; 31–60 in the Partly Free; and 61–100 in the Not Free press group.

Legend

	LEGAL ENVIRONMENT: 0–30 POINTS
	POLITICAL ENVIRONMENT: 0–40 POINTS
Country	ECONOMIC ENVIRONMENT: 0–30 POINTS
Status: Free (0–30)	TOTAL SCORE: 0–100 POINTS
Partly Free (31–60)	
Not Free (61–100)	

Press Freedom in 2003

Karin Deutsch Karlekar

Press freedom worldwide suffered a substantial decline in 2003 as journalists and media outlets faced renewed legal harassment, political pressure, and violence at the hands of both police and security forces and armed insurgent groups. This was the second year in a row that the global level of freedom for news media declined, with the downward trend being particularly noticeable in the Americas and in Central and Eastern Europe and the Former Soviet Union. Of particular concern is the fact that threats to press freedom are occurring not only in authoritarian states but also in faltering democracies and countries in transition. In 2003, even a long-standing democracy such as Italy witnessed a decline in media independence, demonstrating that threats to press freedom are widespread and can emerge in a diverse range of polities.

The annual Freedom House survey of press freedom assesses the degree of print, broadcast, and Internet freedom in every country in the world, analyzing events that take place during each calendar year. Ratings are determined on the basis of an examination of three broad categories: the legal environment in which media operate, political influences on reporting and access to information, and economic pressures on content and the dissemination of news. The survey provides a numerical rating from 0 (the most free) to 100 (the least free) for each country as well as categorizing the level of press freedom as "Free," "Partly Free," or "Not Free" based on each country's numerical rating.

Karin Deutsch Karlekar, a senior researcher at Freedom House, served as managing editor of Freedom of the Press 2004. *She holds a Ph.D. in history from Cambridge University.*

In 2003, out of the 192 countries and 1 territory surveyed, 73 countries (38 percent) were rated Free, while 49 (25 percent) were rated Partly Free and 71 (37 percent) were rated Not Free. The year saw a continued deterioration in press freedom worldwide, as measured by a shift in category. Overall, 5 countries (Bolivia, Bulgaria, Cape Verde, Italy, and the Philippines) declined from Free to Partly Free, while 5 countries (Gabon, Guatemala, Guinea-Bissau, Moldova, and Morocco) declined from Partly Free to Not Free. Only 2 countries—Kenya and Sierra Leone—registered a positive category shift in 2003 from Not Free to Partly Free.

In terms of population, 17 percent of the world's inhabitants live in countries that enjoy a Free press, while 40 percent have a Partly Free press and 43 percent have a Not Free press. This situation represents a considerable decline over the past two years, as the proportion of the world's population able to enjoy access to a Free press has declined by 5 percentage points while the percentage of people who live in countries with a Not Free media environment has also increased by 5 percentage points.

Worryingly, much of this deterioration has taken place in newly established electoral democracies, where a free press is one of a number of necessary components in promoting a vibrant, transparent, and accountable environment. In fragile or emerging democracies, backsliding on a commitment to uphold press freedom can often take place as civic institutions struggle to take root and new leaders unused to scrutiny clamp down on critical or dissenting voices in the media.

In addition, in 2003 the survey noted that a decline had also taken place even in Italy, an established democracy. Long plagued by an inadequate legal and institutional framework and a relatively lower level of press freedom than its European neighbors, Italy was downgraded to Partly Free in 2003 due to an unprecedented concentration of media ownership and a resulting increase in and misuse of political pressure on media outlets. Silvio Berlusconi has used his position as prime minister to exert undue influence over the public broadcaster RAI, in addition to manipulating coverage at his family's own sizable media empire, which includes Italy's three largest private television stations. During the year, a number of claims arose that the government had intervened to exert control over the tenor and type of news coverage. In addition, the editor of a major daily newspaper resigned in May, allegedly under official pressure.

The dangers for press freedom inherent when a media baron turns ruling politician can also be seen in the case of Thailand, which was downgraded in 2002 and showed a continued decline in 2003 as cases of legal harassment and editorial interference with critical news outlets increased during the year. Corporations controlled by Prime Minister Thaksin Shinawatra's family or with ties to the ruling party own or have shares in a growing number of private media outlets and exert influence over editorial policy. Business associates of members of the government also withheld advertisements from news outlets in a further attempt to stifle critical coverage.

Regional Trends

The regional declines noted in 2002 in the cases of the Americas and of Central and Eastern Europe and the Former Soviet Union continued during 2003. In the Americas, 17 countries (49 percent) were rated Free, 13 (37 percent) were rated Partly Free, and 5 (14 percent) were rated Not Free in 2003. Although just under half the countries in the region have media that remain classified as Free, the negative regional trends noted last year continued, with the downgrades of Bolivia to Partly Free and Guatemala to Not Free. During the past two years, the percentage of countries whose media are classified as Free has declined from 60 percent to 49 percent, while the percentage of countries with Not Free media has increased from 6 percent to 14 percent. In Central and Eastern Europe and the Former Soviet Union, the downward trend continued in 2003 as two countries— Bulgaria and Moldova—were downgraded. In this year's survey, 8 countries (30 percent) were classified as Free, 8 (30 percent) as Partly Free, and 11 (40 percent) as Not Free. The situation for the press in Central Asia and, to a lesser extent the Caucasus, remains deeply troubled. Of the former Soviet Union and Soviet bloc countries that remain outside the expanded EU, none are Free, 3 are Partly Free, and 11 are Not Free.

The greatest movement in 2003 took place in Sub-Saharan Africa, where three countries declined in category while two registered positive category shifts. Overall, 7 countries (15 percent) were rated Free, 17 (35 percent) were rated Partly Free, and 24 (50 percent) remain rated Not Free. The overall level of press freedom remained largely unchanged in Europe, Asia, and the Middle East, although one country was downgraded in each region. The region with the worst conditions for the media continued to be the Middle East and North Africa, with 1 country (5 percent) rated Free, 1 (5 percent) rated Partly Free, and 17 (90 percent) rated Not Free. In 2003, Morocco slipped over the cusp to be rated as Not Free, primarily as a result of restrictive anti-terrorist legislation and a legal crackdown on critical media voices.

Western Europe continued to boast the highest level of press freedom worldwide, with 23 countries (92 percent) rated Free and 2 (8 percent) rated Partly Free. Nevertheless, in 2003 Italy joined Turkey as the only countries in the region to be rated as Partly Free. It is the first time since 1988 that the media in an EU member state have been rated by the survey as Partly Free. The Asia Pacific region also exhibited a relatively high level of press freedom, with 17 countries (44 percent) rated Free, 8 (20 percent) rated Partly Free, and 14 (36 percent) rated Not Free. When one examines the figures in terms of population, the outlook is less positive; only seven percent of Asia's population had access to Free media in 2003. However, this is largely due to the fact that China, with its large population, continues to be ranked as Not Free. After being rated as Free for the past six years, the Philippines slipped back into the ranks of the Partly Free countries, largely as the result of a sustained high level of violence against journalists. Afghanistan, which had registered the largest numerical improvement in 2002, remained Not Free in 2003. Despite a continued expansion of independent print and broadcast media outlets, journalists remain subject to legal pressures as well as threats from political and military leaders.

Positive Trends during the Year

Despite the continued downward trend in global press freedom conditions noted above, two positive category shifts did occur in 2003, both in Africa. In Sierra Leone, an official end to the civil war in January 2002 led to a status upgrade this year from Not Free to Partly Free. Although journalists are still subjected to criminal libel charges and other forms of official harassment, an increased level of political stability over the past two years has meant that they are generally able to operate more freely. Similarly in Kenya, under a new government elected in December 2002, the media have demonstrated greater editorial independence and the number of press freedom abuses has decreased, raising Kenya's status from Not Free to Partly Free. Elsewhere in Africa, Angola showed continued signs of improvement as a result of the 2002 signing of an accord between the government and rebel fighters and the consolidation of the peace process over the past year.

However, the year's most dramatic media-environment opening took place in Iraq, which had previously ranked as one of the world's most repressive environments for the press. With the toppling of Saddam Hussein's regime in April 2003, hundreds of new publications covering a wide range of opinions emerged, while Iraqis also gained access to the

Internet and to uncensored foreign broadcasts. Nevertheless, a continuing security vacuum in which at least 13 journalists were killed, coupled with an ambiguous legal and regulatory media framework, meant that Iraq remained in the ranks of the Not Free countries in 2003 despite its impressive gains. [A detailed study of the post-Saddam media environment in Iraq is provided in an essay by Brian Katulis on page 17 of this volume.]

Media Affected by Political Turmoil and Electoral Competition

While upheaval in Iraq led to positive changes for the media, in a number of other countries political turmoil or government crackdowns preceding and during elections had a negative impact on the press. In Bolivia, media outlets became polarized during the course of a mass uprising against the president in October 2003. Journalists faced increased threats and physical harassment from both the government and opposition supporters, which led to a decline in Bolivia's rating to Partly Free. Likewise, in Guatemala journalists were subjected to intensified intimidation prior to and during the November 2003 elections. In an environment in which media outlets already operated under legal restrictions and other forms of official coercion, this additional form of pressure was enough to push Guatemala's rating into the Not Free category. Election-related intimidation and violence against the media was also a concern in Argentina, Azerbaijan, and Guinea during the year.

Even before the campaigning or voting has begun, an impending vote can also spur ruling administrations to crack down on the press. This was the case in Guinea-Bissau, where governmental attempts to silence the opposition's viewpoints in both the public and private media during 2003 led to a status downgrade from Partly Free to Not Free. The country's main independent radio station, Radio Bombolom, was shut in February, while the national radio station's editor-in-chief was assaulted and expelled from his office in March. Meanwhile, officials in Rwanda denied all candidates equal access to media coverage while using the state-run media to lambaste the opposition. Elections scheduled for 2004 prompted campaigns against the independent media during 2003 in Algeria, Cameroon, and Tunisia, mostly in the form of increased legal harassment and pressure. In Ukraine, which is facing important elections in the fall of 2004, concern has been raised that the declining level of media independence noted over the past several years will have a negative impact on press coverage of the campaign and election process. [A more detailed study of the ability of Ukraine's news media to cover the 2004 presidential elections effectively is provided in the essay by Jeremy Druker and Dean Cox on page 29 of this volume.]

New Legislation Threatens the Press

In several countries, new laws passed during the year contributed significantly to a category downgrade. Moldova's rating decreased to Not Free after the government enacted a Law on Combating Extremism, which provided authorities with another possible tool of media repression. In addition, new civil and criminal codes that went into effect in January 2003 contain increasingly harsh penalties for libel, including prison sentences of up to five years. The Moroccan media were also downgraded to Not Free in 2003 due to the controversial passage of a new antiterrorist law in May that reversed many of the press freedoms only recently protected in the 2002 revised press code. Since May, the government has invoked Article 41 of the antiterror legislation to suppress press freedom—setting stricter limits on and penalties for speech offenses—under the pretext of ensuring Moroccan territorial integrity. In Tonga, the king's desire to silence a critical independent newspaper led to the enactment of new legal restrictions on foreign ownership and stringent licensing requirements. Meanwhile, the Zimbabwean government used repressive legislation passed in 2002 to harass the independent press repeatedly during 2003.

Political Influence over the Media on the Rise

The press freedom rating in a number of countries was downgraded in 2003 as a result of increased political pressure, which most often took the form of governmental control of the media (particularly the broadcast media) or official influence over press content. Ruling administrations also attempted to harass the press by bringing politically motivated lawsuits against journalists as well as using restrictive legislation to suspend or close media outlets.

In Bulgaria, the government exerts influence over the press through its control of state broadcasters, a politicized process of allocating licenses, and its practice of rewarding pro-government media outlets with advertising revenue. These practices coupled with a rise in the number of libel suits filed against journalists and publishers caused Bulgaria's rating to drop from Free to Partly Free. Cape Verde was likewise downgraded to Partly Free in 2003, primarily due to convergences in ownership and influence over the media. In Cape Verde's case, the combined facts of state ownership of broadcast media and ruling party control over many private media outlets have led to a decline in editorial independence and a reported increase in self-censorship on the part of journalists.

The government of Gabon made more extreme attempts to exert control over the media, orchestrating a clampdown on the private press that included revoking the licenses of, suspending, or banning a number of private publications. These and other inhibitions on the ability of journalists to work independently led to Gabon's downgrade from Partly Free to Not Free. In Russia, which was downgraded to Not Free in 2002, the situation for the media continued to worsen as the Kremlin consolidated its nearly total control over the broadcast media. Authorities also used legislation and financial pressure to further restrict critical coverage, particularly on sensitive topics such as the war in Chechnya or in the run-up to parliamentary elections held in December.

The numerical scores for Panama and Romania also worsened sharply during 2003 to reflect authorities' increasing use of lawsuits against independent media outlets or critical journalists. In Romania, more than 400 criminal cases were brought against the media during the year, the vast majority concerning defamation, which remains a criminal offense. Most prosecutions resulted in excessive financial penalties or suspended prison sentences. Meanwhile, Panamanian officials frequently invoked repressive press and *desacato* (insult) laws to silence criticism, restrict circulation of information, and create an environment of intimidation and self-censorship among journalists. Currently, over half the members of the media work force have criminal libel or slander cases pending against them.

In the most authoritarian of the world's regimes, flagrant state repression of the media continued unhindered. The five worst-rated countries in 2003 were Burma, Cuba, Libya, North Korea, and Turkmenistan. In these states, independent media are either nonexistent or barely able to operate, the role of the press is to act as a mouthpiece for the ruling regime, and citizens' access to unbiased information is severely limited. After some hints of improvement in 2002, Cuban authorities cracked down on the independent media in March 2003, when 27 journalists were arrested, tried, and sentenced to lengthy prison terms. Press-freedom conditions remained dire in Zimbabwe, Eritrea, and Equatorial Guinea, where authoritarian governments use legal pressure, imprisonment, and other forms of harassment to sharply curtail the ability of independent media outlets to report freely.

Conclusions

As noted above, the level of press freedom worldwide has declined for the second year in a row, and threats to media independence are coming from both democratically elected governments and the world's most repressive states. While authoritarian regimes flagrantly disregard the right of journalists to report freely, political leaders and ruling parties around the world are devising a range of ingenious ways to stifle the media in their own countries as a way of restricting criticism or scrutiny. Representatives from Partly Free and Not Free states are also able to join forces in support of international initiatives that may seek to regulate press freedom. [Some of these, including the UN's World Summit on the Information Society (WSIS), are discussed in greater detail in the essay by Ronald Koven on page 41 of this volume.]

In the current environment, the role of international organizations assumes considerable importance. Groups such as the United Nations, the European Union, and the Council of Europe, as well as lending institutions such as the World Bank, have a potentially vital role to play in terms of setting acceptable standards and holding violators accountable. While these bodies do support initiatives to promote greater media independence, too often they do not offer enough resistance to restrictive efforts, instead acting in a complicit manner. It is important that the statements and actions emanating from these groups offer unequivocal support for press freedom. In this regard, the UN has a special responsibility to ensure that basic standards of press freedom such as Article 19 are not threatened or compromised by initiatives such as the WSIS. Joined by the sustained advocacy efforts of a wide range of freedom-of-expression groups around the world, a clearer message from the international community may go some way to reversing the recent downward trends in media freedom seen during 2003.

GLOBAL AND REGIONAL TABLES

Rank	Country	Rating	Status	Rank	Country	Rating	Status
1	Denmark	8	F		Vanuatu	23	F
	Iceland	8	F	55	Samoa	24	F
	Sweden	8	F		South Africa	24	F
4	Belgium	9	F	57	Nauru	25	F
	Finland	9	F		Papua New Guinea	25	F
	Norway	9	F		Trinidad & Tobago	25	F
	Switzerland	9	F	60	Mauritius	26	F
8	New Zealand	10	F		Uruguay	26	F
9	Palau	11	F	62	Kiribati	27	F
	St. Lucia	11	F		Mali	27	F
11	Liechtenstein	12	F	64	Ghana	28	F
	Luxembourg	12	F		Greece	28	F
	Marshall Islands	12	F		Israel	28	F
	The Netherlands	12	F		Sao Tome & Principe	28	F
15	Andorra	13	F	68	East Timor	29	F
	Monaco	13	F		Fiji	29	F
	United States	13	F		South Korea	29	F
18	Australia	14	F	71	Benin	30	F
	Bahamas	14	F		Botswana	30	F
	Portugal	14	F		Solomon Islands	30	F
	San Marino	14	F	74	Italy	33	PF
	St. Vincent & Grenadines	14	F	75	Namibia	34	PF
23	Canada	15	F		Peru	34	PF
	Malta	15	F		Philippines	34	PF
25	Germany	16	F	78	Argentina	35	PF
	Grenada	16	F		Bulgaria	35	PF
	Ireland	16	F	80	Brazil	36	PF
28	Barbados	17	F		Cape Verde	36	PF
	Dominica	17	F		Mexico	36	PF
	Estonia	17	F		Mongolia	36	PF
	Jamaica	17	F	84	Bolivia	37	PF
	Latvia	17	F		Croatia	37	PF
33	Cyprus	18	F		Nicaragua	37	PF
	Japan	18	F		Senegal	37	PF
	Lithuania	18	F	88	Burkina Faso	39	PF
	Suriname	18	F		Dominican Republic	39	PF
37	Costa Rica	19	F		Thailand	39	PF
	France	19	F	91	Lesotho	40	PF
	Micronesia	19	F		Serbia & Montenegro	40	PF
	Poland	19	F	93	India	41	PF
	Slovenia	19	F		Madagascar	41	PF
	Spain	19	F	95	Ecuador	42	PF
	Tuvalu	19	F		El Salvador	42	PF
	United Kingdom	19	F	97	Antigua & Barbuda	43	PF
45	Guyana	20	F	98	Tonga	44	PF
	Hungary	20	F		Uganda	44	PF
47	St. Kitts & Nevis	21	F	100	Comoros	45	PF
	Slovakia	21	F		Mozambique	45	PF
49	Belize	22	F		Panama	45	PF
50	Austria	23	F	103	Romania	47	PF
	Chile	23	F	104	Bosnia-Herzegovina	48	PF
	Czech Republic	23	F	105	Albania	49	PF
	Taiwan	23	F	106	Tanzania	50	PF

Table of Global Press Freedom Rankings

Rank	Country	Rating	Status	Rank	Country	Rating	Status
107	Honduras	52	PF		Venezuela	68	NF
	Malawi	52	PF	154	Malaysia	69	NF
	Seychelles	52	PF	155	Bahrain	70	NF
	Turkey	52	PF	156	Azerbaijan	71	NF
111	Macedonia	53	PF		Guinea	71	NF
	Nigeria	53	PF		Kyrgyzstan	71	NF
	Sri Lanka	53	PF	159	Afghanistan	72	NF
114	Congo (Brazzaville)	54	PF	160	Tajikistan	73	NF
	Georgia	54	PF	161	Brunei	74	NF
	Paraguay	54	PF		Chad	74	NF
117	Indonesia	55	PF		Kazakhstan	74	NF
118	Niger	56	PF		Oman	74	NF
119	Kuwait	57	PF	165	Burundi	75	NF
120	Sierra Leone	58	PF		Liberia	75	NF
121	Pakistan	59	PF		United Arab Emirates	75	NF
122	Kenya	60	PF	168	Egypt	76	NF
123	Morocco	61	NF	169	Swaziland	77	NF
	Qatar	61	NF	170	Togo	78	NF
125	Gabon	62	NF	171	Haiti	79	NF
	Guatemala	62	NF		Iran	79	NF
127	Algeria	63	NF	173	China	80	NF
	Cambodia	63	NF		Congo (Kinshasa)	80	NF
	Colombia	63	NF		Saudi Arabia	80	NF
	The Gambia	63	NF		Somalia	80	NF
	Guinea-Bissau	63	NF		Syria	80	NF
	Jordan	63	NF		Tunisia	80	NF
	Moldova	63	NF	179	Laos	82	NF
	Zambia	63	NF		Rwanda	82	NF
135	Armenia	64	NF		Vietnam	82	NF
	Central African Republic	64	NF	182	Belarus	84	NF
	Maldives	64	NF		Uzbekistan	84	NF
	Mauritania	64	NF	184	Sudan	85	NF
	Singapore	64	NF	185	IAT/PA*	86	NF
140	Cote d'Ivoire	65	NF	186	Equatorial Guinea	89	NF
	Nepal	65	NF		Eritrea	89	NF
142	Angola	66	NF		Zimbabwe	89	NF
	Djibouti	66	NF	189	Libya	94	NF
	Ethiopia	66	NF	190	Burma	95	NF
	Iraq	66	NF		Turkmenistan	95	NF
	Lebanon	66	NF	192	Cuba	96	NF
147	Cameroon	67	NF	193	North Korea	98	NF
	Russia	67	NF				
	Yemen	67	NF	*Israeli Administered Territories/			
150	Bangladesh	68	NF		Palestinian Authority		
	Bhutan	68	NF				
	Ukraine	68	NF		F=Free / PF=Partly Free / NF=Not Free		

Status	Number of countries	Percent of total
Free	73	38%
Partly Free	49	25%
Not Free	71	37%
TOTAL	193	100%

11

Press Freedom Rankings by Region

Sub-Saharan Africa

Rank	Country	Rating	Status	Rank	Country	Rating	Status
1	South Africa	24	F	25	Gabon	62	NF
2	Mauritius	26	F	26	The Gambia	63	NF
3	Mali	27	F		Guinea-Bissau	63	NF
4	Ghana	28	F		Zambia	63	NF
	Sao Tome & Principe	28	F	29	Central African Republic	64	NF
6	Benin	30	F		Mauritania	64	NF
	Botswana	30	F	31	Cote d'Ivoire	65	NF
8	Namibia	34	PF	32	Angola	66	NF
9	Cape Verde	36	PF		Djibouti	66	NF
10	Senegal	37	PF		Ethiopia	66	NF
11	Burkina Faso	39	PF	35	Cameroon	67	NF
12	Lesotho	40	PF	36	Guinea	71	NF
13	Madagascar	41	PF	37	Chad	74	NF
14	Uganda	44	PF	38	Burundi	75	NF
15	Comoros	45	PF		Liberia	75	NF
	Mozambique	45	PF	40	Swaziland	77	NF
17	Tanzania	50	PF	41	Togo	78	NF
18	Malawi	52	PF	42	Congo (Kinshasa)	80	NF
	Seychelles	52	PF		Somalia	80	NF
20	Nigeria	53	PF	44	Rwanda	82	NF
21	Congo (Brazzaville)	54	PF	45	Sudan	85	NF
22	Niger	56	PF	46	Equatorial Guinea	89	NF
23	Sierra Leone	58	PF		Eritrea	89	NF
24	Kenya	60	PF		Zimbabwe	89	NF

Status	Number of countries	Percent of total
Free	7	15%
Partly Free	17	35%
Not Free	24	50%
TOTAL	48	100%

Americas

Rank	Country	Rating	Status	Rank	Country	Rating	Status
1	St. Lucia	11	F	19	Argentina	35	PF
2	United States	13	F	20	Brazil	36	PF
3	Bahamas	14	F		Mexico	36	PF
	St. Vincent & Grenadines	14	F	22	Bolivia	37	PF
5	Canada	15	F		Nicaragua	37	PF
6	Grenada	16	F	24	Dominican Republic	39	PF
7	Barbados	17	F	25	Ecuador	42	PF
	Dominica	17	F		El Salvador	42	PF
	Jamaica	17	F	27	Antigua & Barbuda	43	PF
10	Suriname	18	F	28	Panama	45	PF
11	Costa Rica	19	F	29	Honduras	52	PF
12	Guyana	20	F	30	Paraguay	54	PF
13	St. Kitts & Nevis	21	F	31	Guatemala	62	NF
14	Belize	22	F	32	Colombia	63	NF
15	Chile	23	F	33	Venezuela	68	NF
16	Trinidad & Tobago	25	F	34	Haiti	79	NF
17	Uruguay	26	F	35	Cuba	96	NF
18	Peru	34	PF				

Status	Number of countries	Percent of total
Free	17	49%
Partly Free	13	37%
Not Free	5	14%
TOTAL	35	100%

Middle East & North Africa

Rank	Country	Rating	Status	Rank	Country	Rating	Status
1	Israel	28	F	12	United Arab Emirates	75	NF
2	Kuwait	57	PF	13	Egypt	76	NF
3	Morocco	61	NF	14	Iran	79	NF
	Qatar	61	NF	15	Saudi Arabia	80	NF
5	Algeria	63	NF		Syria	80	NF
	Jordan	63	NF	17	Tunisia	80	NF
7	Iraq	66	NF	18	IAT/PA*	86	NF
	Lebanon	66	NF	19	Libya	94	NF
9	Yemen	67	NF				
10	Bahrain	70	NF	*Israeli Administered Territories/			
11	Oman	74	NF	Palestinian Authority			

Status	Number of countries	Percent of total
Free	1	5%
Partly Free	1	5%
Not Free	17	90%
TOTAL	19	100%

Asia-Pacific

Rank	Country	Rating	Status	Rank	Country	Rating	Status
1	New Zealand	10	F	21	India	41	PF
2	Palau	11	F	22	Tonga	44	PF
3	Marshall Islands	12	F	23	Sri Lanka	53	PF
4	Australia	14	F	24	Indonesia	55	PF
5	Japan	18	F	25	Pakistan	59	PF
6	Micronesia	19	F	26	Cambodia	63	NF
	Tuvalu	19	F	27	Maldives	64	NF
8	Taiwan	23	F		Singapore	64	NF
	Vanuatu	23	F	29	Nepal	65	NF
10	Samoa	24	F	30	Bangladesh	68	NF
11	Nauru	25	F		Bhutan	68	NF
	Papua New Guinea	25	F	32	Malaysia	69	NF
13	Kiribati	27	F	33	Afghanistan	72	NF
14	East Timor	29	F	34	Brunei	74	NF
	Fiji	29	F	35	China	80	NF
	South Korea	29	F	36	Laos	82	NF
17	Solomon Islands	30	F		Vietnam	82	NF
18	Philippines	34	PF	38	Burma	95	NF
19	Mongolia	36	PF	39	North Korea	98	NF
20	Thailand	39	PF				

Status	Number of countries	Percent of total
Free	17	44%
Partly Free	8	20%
Not Free	14	36%
TOTAL	39	100%

14

Western Europe

Rank	Country	Rating	Status	Rank	Country	Rating	Status
1	Denmark	8	F	13	Portugal	14	F
	Iceland	8	F		San Marino	14	F
	Sweden	8	F	15	Malta	15	F
4	Belgium	9	F	16	Germany	16	F
	Finland	9	F		Ireland	16	F
	Norway	9	F	18	Cyprus	18	F
	Switzerland	9	F	19	France	19	F
8	Liechtenstein	12	F		Spain	19	F
	Luxembourg	12	F		United Kingdom	19	F
	Netherlands	12	F	22	Austria	23	F
11	Andorra	13	F	23	Greece	28	F
	Monaco	13	F	24	Italy	33	PF
				25	Turkey	52	PF

Status	Number of countries	Percent of total
Free	23	92%
Partly Free	2	8%
Not Free	0	0%
TOTAL	25	100%

Central and Eastern Europe / Former Soviet Union

Rank	Country	Rating	Status	Rank	Country	Rating	Status
1	Estonia	17	F	15	Macedonia	53	PF
	Latvia	17	F	16	Georgia	54	PF
3	Lithuania	18	F	17	Moldova	63	NF
4	Poland	19	F	18	Armenia	64	NF
	Slovenia	19	F	19	Russia	67	NF
6	Hungary	20	F	20	Ukraine	68	NF
7	Slovakia	21	F	21	Azerbaijan	71	NF
8	Czech Republic	23	F		Kyrgyzstan	71	NF
9	Bulgaria	35	PF	23	Tajikistan	73	NF
10	Croatia	37	PF	24	Kazakhstan	74	NF
11	Serbia & Montenegro	40	PF	25	Belarus	84	NF
12	Romania	47	PF		Uzbekistan	84	NF
13	Bosnia-Herzegovina	48	PF	27	Turkmenistan	95	NF
14	Albania	49	PF				

Status	Number of countries	Percent of total
Free	8	30%
Partly Free	8	30%
Not Free	11	40%
TOTAL	27	100%

Summary of Results

Regional Press Freedom Breakdown

Region	Free	Partly Free	Not Free	Number of Countries
Americas	17 (49%)	13 (37%)	5 (14%)	35
Asia-Pacific	17 (44%)	8 (20%)	14 (36%)	39
CEE/FSU	8 (30%)	8 (30%)	11 (40%)	27
Middle East & North Africa	1 (5%)	1 (5%)	17 (90%)	19
Sub-Saharan Africa	7 (15%)	17 (35%)	24 (50%)	48
Western Europe	23 (92%)	2 (8%)	0 (0%)	25
TOTAL	73 (38%)	49 (25%)	71 (37%)	193

Press Freedom by Population

Status	By Country	By Population (millions)
Free	73 (38%)	1,086 (17%)
Partly Free	49 (25%)	2,520 (40%)
Not Free	71 (37%)	2,693 (43%)
TOTAL	193 (100%)	6,299 (100%)

Liberated and Occupied Iraq: New Beginnings and Challenges for Press Freedom

Brian Katulis

The collapse of Saddam Hussein's repressive regime in April 2003 sparked a historic media boom in Iraq in the months that followed. Hundreds of new publications and television and radio channels emerged in what turned out to be an unparalleled media free-for-all involving a broad range of Iraqi and regional media forces. A massive increase in the numbers of satellite dishes—banned under Saddam Hussein—opened Iraqis up to new sources of information. Access to the Internet, which had been tightly controlled under the Hussein regime, flourished as Internet cafes sprang up all over the country. A year after the fall of Saddam Hussein's government, analysts estimated that more than 200 newspapers and 90 television and radio stations were operating in Iraq, representing an unprecedented diversity of media in that country. However, the quality of these new publications and media outlets has been uneven.

In this expanded, more diverse and complex media environment, the U.S.-led Coalition Provisional Authority (CPA) set into motion plans to

Brian Katulis is an opinion research consultant who has worked on democratic development projects throughout the Middle East. In 2003, he organized one of the first nationwide opinion research projects in Iraq for the National Democratic Institute for International Affairs (NDI). His previous experience includes work at Greenberg Quinlan Rosner Research, the Policy Planning Staff at the Department of State, the National Security Council, and NDI.

transform and regulate Iraq's media. The CPA's first action was to issue a decree banning media activities aimed at inciting violence and spreading instability. Working with its Iraqi interim governing partners, the CPA invoked this decree a number of times, permanently shutting down a handful of publications and temporarily banning some media outlets in an attempt to balance press freedom with stability and order. U.S.-led efforts to create a new national media network faced many setbacks in late 2003 and early 2004, but by March 2004 the CPA had formally issued decrees setting up a new national media network and establishing regulatory bodies for the media.

The ongoing conflict and instability that continue to plague Iraq represent one of the greatest threats to Iraq's newfound press freedoms. The year following the fall of Saddam was dangerous and sometimes deadly for journalists and other media professionals working in Iraq: By the spring of 2004, nearly two dozen media professionals had been killed and scores more wounded in attacks. Some press casualties resulted from journalists' being caught in crossfire, while others were due to directed and politically motivated attacks. Continued uncertainty about the CPA's transfer of political authority back to Iraq, which occurred on June 28, 2004, loomed as an additional challenge for press freedom. Even post-handover, the lack of clarity about Iraq's future political and legal structures raises questions about whether the press freedoms gained since the removal of Saddam Hussein's regime will endure without strong protections, impartial regulation, and clear journalistic standards.

Before Liberation:
Saddam Hussein's Brutal Domination of the Press

The ouster of Saddam Hussein in April 2003 ended a reign of fear in which the Iraqi government maintained complete and brutal control over the media. For nearly three decades, official government propaganda dominated media coverage in Iraq, with few openings for voices and sources of information independent of the Iraqi government.

Restrictions on press freedom pre-date Saddam Hussein's rule, as the Baathist revolution in 1968 brought with it censorship and restrictions on media that had once been considered among the freest and most diverse in the Middle East. However, when Saddam Hussein took over Iraq's presidency in 1979, he moved further to crush the few political opponents and independent media voices that remained. By the mid-1980s, the ruling Baath Party and Saddam Hussein's family had established a complete monopoly on the media. In 1986, Iraq's ruling Revolutionary Command Council issued Order Number 840, which imposed the death penalty on anyone who criticized or insulted the president. Authorities used brute force to quash independent and opposition views; appalling acts, such as cutting out the tongues of journalists who strayed from official propaganda, were common, and hundreds of journalists and authors are thought to have been killed by the regime.

Saddam Hussein's son Uday was head of the Iraqi Journalist Union, a mandatory union for all Iraqi journalists. Assuming this leadership position in 1992 at the early age of 27, Uday Hussein exercised complete control over all television and radio stations and managed about a dozen newspapers, including *Babel*, the most widely read publication in Iraq.

As Iraq's war with Iran raged from 1980 to 1988, Iraq's media grew increasingly insular, and the country lost touch with the information revolution starting to sweep over most parts of the globe. The regime banned satellite dishes, punishing violators with up to six months in prison and fines, and jammed signals from broadcasters attempting to offer alternative views and information from outside Iraq. Iraq was one of the last countries to link up to the Internet, and when it was finally introduced in the late 1990s all access was controlled by the government's Internet server. Moreover, Iraq's ministry of information blocked access to many Web sites and permitted e-mail only from Iraq-based servers that copied messages to the government. Government security services closely monitored foreign journalists and limited their independent access to the public, obscuring the scale and scope of Saddam Hussein's atrocities in reports to the outside world. Foreign newspapers were prohibited inside Iraq.

There were exceptions to the Hussein regime's total control of the media, particularly after the 1991 Gulf War. The Kurdish north, which from 1991 on lived under the protection of a U.S.-enforced no-fly zone that prevented Saddam Hussein from exercising control over those territories, saw a flourishing media emerge in the 1990s. In addition, outside broadcasters, including Radio Sawa, Radio Monte Carlo, the British Broadcasting Corporation (BBC), and Voice of America, began to have increasing success at reaching broader segments of the Iraqi public. However, despite these limited pockets of press freedom, when the war began in 2003, most Iraqis were living in a fog of disinformation dominated by Saddam Hussein's official propaganda. As the war commenced, the Iraqi regime initiated a number of final desperate attempts to control the media, influence Iraqi opinion, and skew international coverage. Hundreds of international journalists were in Iraq to cover the war, but they remained subject to Iraqi government control and supervision. According to a report by Reporters Without Borders, Iraqi authorities arrested at least 10 journalists in late March 2003 for alleged visa irregularities.

The official Iraqi media operated intermittently during the war, broadcasting messages favorable to Saddam Hussein and seeking to cast doubt on the effectiveness of the Coalition forces' military campaign. Perhaps the Hussein regime's most infamous attempt to influence public views on the war came from regular press conferences held by Iraqi Information Minister Mohammed Saeed Al-Sahaf, who achieved cult status for his denials and often nonsensical statements contradicting reality. Despite credible reporting from multiple sources that Coalition forces had reached Baghdad, Al-Sahaf continued to make statements like, "I triple guarantee you—there are no American soldiers in Baghdad." Though the Iraqi military for the most part offered limited and sporadic resistance during the war, Al-Sahaf once said, "We're giving them a real lesson today. Heavy doesn't accurately describe the level of casualties we have inflicted." Al-Sahaf's press conferences and statements became an anachronistic symbol of a regime that continued to try to control information in its dying days.

Iraq's Media Boom of 2003–2004

Iraq enjoyed a historic media boom in the months that followed the collapse of Saddam Hussein's regime in April 2003, with a spike in the number of satellite dishes, people with Internet access, and media outlets. Analysts estimate that more than 200 newspapers and magazines appeared in Iraq, although according to the BBC less than half of those publications survived the first year. Iraq also had more than 90 television and radio stations a year after Saddam Hussein's removal from power.

These new media reflect the broad array of opinions and views that previously were either crushed or co-opted by Saddam Hussein's government. Sunni and Shiite clerics, Kurdish activists, communists, democratic liberals, unaffiliated satirists, and other voices not heard for decades set up new newspapers and magazines. Around the country, local television and radio stations sprang up. In the holy cities of Najaf and Karbala, the local television outlets tended to place greater emphasis on religious programming.

In the context of this newfound freedom, two main criticisms emerged in the immediate postwar period. First, several critics pointed to a dearth of independent and objective sources of information; many of the new media outlets were set up by new political groups and parties, and their reporting was biased in favor of promoting their parties' leaders and achievements rather than objectively reporting on events. Second, several media observers noted that the new Iraqi press suffered from a lack of clear journalistic standards. The quality of reporting in several Iraqi publications and media outlets was uneven, with sensationalistic tabloids reporting unsubstantiated rumors and conspiracy theories that at times had the potential for inflaming passions and sparking violence.

This is not to say that all of the new Iraqi media were plagued by partisan views or low professional standards. Numerous examples exist in which responsible reporting by Iraqi journalists contributed positively to public debate and greater transparency. For example, in January 2004, *Al-Mada*, a small Baghdad-based newspaper with a circulation of about 5,000, gained credibility for naming dozens of individuals who allegedly received oil bribes in return for supporting Saddam Hussein.

In addition to the massive increase in the number of Iraqi publications and media outlets, regional media forces entered the fray. Two regional Arab satellite television channels, Al-Arabiya and Al-Jazeera, garnered a great deal of attention inside and outside Iraq, presenting the CPA and interim Iraqi governing officials with many challenges related to balancing press freedom with responsible reporting.

Iranian-sponsored media outlets have gained greater prominence as well. The official Islamic Republic of Iran Broadcasting Radio Channel can be heard in Baghdad, and the Arabic language Voice of the Mujahideen (Holy Fighters) of the Supreme Council for the Islamic Revolution in Iraq (SCIRI), an Iraqi Shiite group, receives support from Iran. In addition, two Iranian television stations, Sahar and Al-Alam, have joined the ever-growing list of media options for ordinary Iraqis.

Entering the media competition, the United States in February 2004 established a regional satellite television station named Al-Hurra—a publicly funded, 24-hour Arabic-language news and information channel. Meanwhile, entrepreneurs have seen the expanding press freedom and open system as a good business opportunity. For example, in the spring of 2004, Naguib Sawiris, an Egyptian media magnate, announced plans to start Al-Hawa, a private television channel, to compete with other broadcasters.

Challenges in Rebuilding Iraq's Media
and Setting Up a New Regulatory Framework

Responsibility for overseeing postwar reconstruction in Iraq fell into the hands of the newly created CPA, headed by former U.S. Ambassador L. Paul Bremer III. The efforts to rebuild Iraq's media and set up a new regulatory framework encountered problems similar to those faced in other areas of Iraq's reconstruction. They were hampered by ongoing instability and violence in the country, ambiguity about the CPA's longer-term vision for the country, uncertainty about Iraq's future political structures, and wrangling between different Iraqi political forces.

Though a lack of clarity existed as to how the CPA was legally constituted—with some pointing to United Nations Resolution 1483 as the legal justification and others citing U.S. National Security Presidential Directives that were not publicly released—in May 2003 the CPA became the de facto entity that exercised temporary powers of government and was to manage the transfer of political authority back to Iraq. The CPA reported to the U.S. Department of Defense, and the decrees it issued became law. In July 2003, the CPA created the Iraqi Governing Council (IGC), a body of 25 Iraqis that served the U.S.-led coalition in a largely advisory capacity.

CPA's Order 14 and Challenges Balancing Press Freedom with Responsible Journalism. The CPA had primary responsibility for establishing the new legal and regulatory framework for Iraq's media; one of its earliest actions was to issue a new decree on the media. On June 10, 2003, the CPA issued Order 14, which set some basic rules for the media and prohibited media activities aimed at inciting violence, civil disorder, rioting, or action against Coalition forces or the CPA. In addition, Order 14 banned the media from advocating changes to Iraq's borders by any means or advocating a return to power of the Iraqi Baath Party. Order 14 gave Ambassador Bremer the sole authority to close media organizations; the only process set up for media organizations to protest a closure by the CPA was a written appeal with evidence to that same CPA Administrator, Ambassador Bremer.

CPA officials said that the main objective of the order was to enhance civil stability and prevent irresponsible journalists from inflaming an already volatile and tenuous situation. Critics of the order expressed concerns that it could open the door to arbitrary and unnecessary censorship.

CPA Order 14 was cited to justify the closure or temporary ban of a number of newspapers and media outlets. One of the earliest instances of its implementation came in July 2003, when U.S. troops and Iraqi police raided the Baghdad offices of the *Al-Mustaqila* newspaper and detained the newspaper's manager, Abdul Sattar Shalan. CPA officials said that *Al-Mustaqila* had published an article proclaiming the killing of spies who cooperate with the United States to be a religious duty, echoing messages issued by armed groups who had been conducting attacks against Coalition forces.

The general guidelines set out by Order 14 were also referenced by U.S. and interim Iraqi governing council officials as justification for temporary bans and restrictions on coverage by the Arab satellite television channels Al-Jazeera and Al-Arabiya. Both channels were repeatedly barred from covering official sessions of the IGC throughout late 2003 and early 2004, and U.S. government and military officials at times accused the channels of working in concert with armed Iraqi groups opposed to the U.S.-led occupation. For example, in the fall of 2003, IGC member Iyad Allawi blamed both channels for inciting violence against IGC members, specifically referring to the murder of IGC member Akila al-Hashimi in September 2003. The IGC also imposed a temporary ban on Al-Arabiya after it broadcast an audiotape by Saddam Hussein in which the former president called for the murders of IGC members and attacks on Coalition forces. IGC member Jalal Talabani asserted that the broadcast stepped over the line of responsible journalism.

The CPA's suspension on March 28, 2004, of *Al-Hawza*, a weekly newspaper controlled by the political movement of firebrand Shiite cleric Muqtada Al-Sadr, stood out among the CPA's efforts to maintain a balance between press freedom and public security. The CPA alleged that *Al-Hawza*'s coverage irresponsibly assigned U.S. helicopters blame for the deaths of more than 50 Iraqi police recruits in a suicide truck bombing on February 10. In addition, CPA Administrator Paul Bremer reportedly objected to the newspaper's editorial comparisons between himself and Saddam Hussein. The closure of *Al-Hawza*, in addition to an announcement that Coalition forces and Iraqi police were seeking to arrest Al-Sadr for his alleged involvement in the murder of a Shiite leader in Najaf in April 2003, sparked protests that led to unrest and conflict that continued through the spring of 2004.

Shaky Efforts to Develop Iraq's New National Media. In the spring of 2003, CPA officials set forth a goal of creating a new national media outlet for Iraq modeled after the BBC and National Public Radio. The CPA brought in Simon Haselock, who had worked for the United Nations in post-conflict situations such as Kosovo and Bosnia-Herzegovina, to serve as head of media development and regulation for the CPA. The CPA also created a national media umbrella organization called the Iraqi Media Network (IMN), comprising the daily newspaper *Al-Sabah*, the national television channel Al-Iraqiyah, and a radio network.

The United States government awarded the initial contract for rebuilding Iraq's media to Science Applications International Corporation (SAIC), a government contractor that specializes in providing advanced technologies to support military operations. SAIC had experience in setting up radio and television transmitters and other equipment required for building a new national media network, but it had less experience in training broadcast and print journalists, a key part of its contract. In the early months, the IMN suffered from staff and management turnovers, poor ratings, and accusations that it was a propaganda tool of the CPA. Ahmed Al-Rikabi, news director at the IMN, resigned in August 2003, citing IMN's under-funding and a lack of independence from the CPA. In a letter to the Associated Press, former adviser and trainer for Al-Iraqiyah Don North wrote that "IMN has become an irrelevant mouthpiece for CPA propaganda, managed news and mediocre foreign programs."

SAIC's inadequate experience for training and managing Iraqi media personnel emerged in media reports on efforts to rebuild Iraq's national press. Iraqi employees of the new media effort alleged that SAIC managers told them to stop conducting man-on-the-street interviews because they were too critical of the American occupation; other Iraqi journalists alleged that they received instructions from their superiors to exclude readings of the Koran from the television channel's cultural programming. IMN television and radio programs were prepared and recorded in the Convention Center in the Green Zone next to the headquarters of the CPA in Baghdad. The choice of location for the network contributed to criticism that IMN reporters were overly isolated and out of touch with rapidly changing events, as well as being constrained from acting independently.

Criticisms of the IMN increased during the fall of 2003. *The Washington Post* called it "psyops [psychological operations] on steroids" in October. The next month, leaders of SCIRI threatened protests, bans, and religious decrees or fatwas against the IMN, alleging that it aired immoral programming. A November 2003 inspection by Pentagon contracting officials found that SAIC had not lived up to many of its contractual obligations, and Congressional officials started to demand a change in course.

In January 2004, Harris Corporation, a U.S. producer of communications equipment, became the new contractor responsible for developing the IMN. Working in cooperation with the Lebanese Broadcasting Corporation (LBC) and the Kuwaiti publishing and telecommunications company Al-Fawares, and with assistance from Microsoft, Harris Corporation set out to correct many of the problems plaguing the CPA's efforts to establish the new national Iraqi media effort. In an attempt to provide a stronger legal basis and structure for the attempts to build the IMN, the CPA issued Order Number 66 on March 20, 2004, which formalized the IMN and established Iraq Public Service Broadcasting, a new national media entity with a board of governors, a financial committee, and a director general.

However, setbacks continued to plague the efforts to build the IMN through the spring of 2004. In March, the IMN newspaper *Al-Sabah* was criticized by a competing newspaper, *Al-Mutamar,* of the Iraqi National Congress, for receiving exclusive contracts and subsidies from Iraqi government ministries. In early May 2004, most of the Iraqi staff of *Al-Sabah* walked out in protest against the lack of editorial independence from the CPA and concerns that its attempts to become a private newspaper would be stifled by the new national media structures established by the CPA in April 2004.

The efforts to reach more Iraqis through the IMN television station Al-Iraqiya had made some progress by the spring of 2004. Television is the medium that has the broadest impact in the country; a nationwide survey conducted in Iraq by CNN, USA Today, and Gallup from March 22 to April 9, 2004, found that 95 percent of Iraqis had a working television set in their home. Moreover, the poll found that three quarters (74 percent) of the public had watched Al-Iraqiya in the past seven days, making it the most- watched television channel in Iraq. Al-Jazeera and Al-Arabiya were watched by a little over one quarter of the public. CPA officials working to develop the IMN pointed to the strong market-share numbers as a sign of success. In addition, nationwide polls conducted by Oxford Research International demonstrated growing confidence in IMN's television channel. By February 2004, fully 50 percent of the Iraqi public expressed confidence in the IMN television channel, up 11 points from November 2003.

However, other analysts noted that Al-Iraqiya had the inherent advantage of being the only national land-based broadcaster, as satellite dishes are not as common as televisions. Furthermore, critics pointed to polling conducted by the U.S. Department of State that showed a small decline in Al-Iraqiya's viewership from the fall of 2003 to the spring of 2004.

In addition, although the land-based Al-Iraqiya was more accessible, the March–April 2004 CNN/USA Today/Gallup opinion research poll indicated that the Iraqi public ranked it lower than Al-Jazeera and Al-Arabiya as being a channel that is bold, unbiased, objective, and the first to break the news.

Establishing a New Regulatory Body for Iraq's Media. In preparation for the transfer of political authority back to Iraq on June 30, 2004, the CPA began to establish structures intended to create the framework for regulating the Iraqi media. In March 2004, the CPA issued Order Number 65, which established the Iraq Communications and Media Commission (ICMC) as an independent, nonprofit administrative institution responsible for licensing and regulating the media, telecommunications, broadcasting, and information services. CPA Administrator Bremer appointed Dr. Siyamend Zaid Othman, a former Amnesty International researcher, as the chief executive officer; Bremer then selected three ICMC commissioners in April 2004. The ICMC is chartered to set new professional standards and codes of conduct for media professionals, establish policies for radio-frequency management, and license all media and telecommunications operations. Its primary task is to propose a new Communications and Broadcasting Law to the future sovereign Iraqi government.

When the CPA announced its visions for the ICMC, *Al-Sabah* criticized the ICMC as being more powerful than the ministry of information under Saddam Hussein. Iraq's interim minister of communications, Haider al-Abadi, who was appointed by the CPA, complained that the ICMC replaced him and that CPA officials had not kept him apprised of the plans for the ICMC as they developed. Other analysts worried that the ICMC set a dangerous new precedent that might encourage the new Iraqi government to dominate and control the private media outlets that have emerged since the fall of Saddam Hussein.

Besides the steps taken by the CPA to build a new national media network and set up a new legal and regulatory framework for the Iraqi press, questions remained about the overall plan for the future. Some analysts pointed out that obsolete laws from the Saddam Hussein era technically remained on the books; for example, Iraqi law 433, which deals with libel, has been used by various individuals to take reporters to court.

Ongoing Violence and Conflict: The Greatest Threat to Press Freedom in Iraq

On the heels of the transfer of political authority from the CPA to Iraq, one of the greatest threats to press freedom is the ongoing violence and general lack of law and order. Although the 2003 war in Iraq and removal of Saddam Hussein have resulted in a historic burgeoning of press freedom, the war and the ongoing conflict have at the same time proved deadly for more than two dozen journalists and media professionals. According to Reporters Without Borders, 12 media professionals were killed in 2003 and 13 were killed in the first four months of 2004.

During the war, U.S. forces were responsible for the deaths of a number of journalists. On April 8, 2003, a shell fired by a U.S. tank at the Palestine Hotel in central Baghdad killed Reuters cameraman Taras Protsyuk and Jose Couso of Spanish television channel Telecinco. U.S. troops maintained that they were returning hostile fire from the hotel, and an investigation by the U.S. military deemed the tank unit's actions a "proportionate and justifiably measured response." On the same day, an American warplane bombed an electricity generator outside the Baghdad bureau of Al-Jazeera, killing reporter Tareq Ayyoub.

During the period of the U.S.-led occupation, Coalition military forces have been responsible for the deaths of a number of other journalists and media professionals. For example, outside the infamous Abu Ghraib prison on the outskirts of Baghdad, U.S. soldiers shot dead Mazen Dana, a Palestinian cameraman working with Reuters. The soldiers said they mistakenly believed that Dana, who had been filming footage, was aiming a rocket-propelled grenade launcher at them. On March 18, 2004, Coalition forces shot and killed two Iraqi journalists working for Al-Arabiya television at a checkpoint in Baghdad; the episode prompted a number of Iraqi journalists to walk out of a news conference held by U.S. Secretary of State Colin Powell. In some cases, the incidents in which Coalition forces killed journalists can be viewed as unfortunate instances not unusual in a volatile and confused environment of conflict. But in other cases, serious questions remain about the judgment and actions of Coalition forces.

Journalists face an even greater threat from armed groups and factions opposed to the U.S.-led coalition, remnants of Saddam Hussein's regime, and common criminals. Incidents of drive-by shootings, bomb attacks, kidnappings, and robberies increased through the fall of 2003 and spring of 2004.

The overall level of instability led to serious ethical questions for news organizations about the best way to protect their journalists working in Iraq. A *Wall Street Journal* report that *New York Times* reporter Dexter Filkins had been traveling in Iraq with a gun set off a debate about appropriate behavior for journalists operating in a conflict and whether armed journalists deprived themselves of their traditional status as noncombatant neutrals. Network television stations employ teams of guards to protect their offices and equipment, but many journalists refuse to arm themselves, fearing that such measures would endanger their ability to report on events.

The great gains in press freedom seen since the fall of Saddam Hussein's regime give hope for Iraq's future. Nevertheless, continuing violence poses the greatest short-term threat to the work of journalists in the country. In the long-term, political instability and the ambiguous legal framework will need to be resolved in order for Iraq's media to truly function freely.

Under Assault: Ukraine's News Media and the 2004 Presidential Elections

Jeremy Druker and Dean Cox

No one should underestimate the political, social, and economic importance of the presidential election scheduled in Ukraine for October 2004. It is clear that this election offers an important opportunity for a new beginning for Ukraine, a country mired in official corruption. Yet given Ukraine's recent history, including its last presidential and parliamentary elections, the next four months do not bode well for the independence of the country's news media. President Leonid Kuchma (who under Ukraine's constitution cannot run for a third term) and his allies will look to secure at all costs the victory of a chosen successor. The election of an opposition candidate could portend a sea change in the upper echelons of power and enable sorely needed reform of the political system.

In the past, analysts in Ukraine and news media watchdog organizations outside this east European country have criticized Ukraine's news media for performing poorly and failing to provide fair political and electoral information to the voting public. The financial dependency of the media and strict control of media companies by the ruling regime, local and

Jeremy Druker, who has written extensively on the news media in post-Soviet Europe, was one of the founders of Transitions Online (TOL) in 1999 and serves as its director and editor-in-chief. Dean C.K. Cox, a New York–based freelance journalist and photojournalist, is a former Knight International Press Fellow with Transitions Online. This essay was originally released as a Freedom House special report in October 2003; the section on events since January 2004 was provided by Jeremy Druker.

regional administrations, and political parties have increased dramatically since President Kuchma's 1999 reelection and intensified during the 2002 parliamentary elections, when intimidation of reporters and media outlets reached its highest point since the consolidation of Ukraine's post-communist independence.

Given the immense implications of a change in state power and the strong showing of opposition forces in recent polls, there is a danger that many news media outlets—particularly broadcast media—will outdo even their past efforts to skew the news agenda. Once again, they can be expected to advance the biased political or business interests of their patrons rather than present a balanced and fair overview of the full range of candidates and their policies.

The administration of President Kuchma, and the United Ukraine and SDPU (united) parties in particular, have learned that a firm grip of the Fourth Estate confers tremendous power. In a depressed economic environment in which many voters cannot afford to buy print media and receive news exclusively from television, the pro-Kuchma forces have established firm control over all national television broadcasters. Many observers interviewed for this report expect Ukraine's past practice of state-controlled media promoting the candidates of incumbent power to continue, while privately owned media engage in a quid pro quo of promoting and attempting to secure the election of a candidate from the ruling elite in return for economic favoritism, political protection, and potential subsidies for economically unprofitable news outlets.

The Last Time Around: Parliamentary Elections in 2002

A look at Ukraine's last national parliamentary elections provides clear evidence of a pattern of direct and indirect state interference in the media's dissemination of alternative and opposition views. According to an OSCE/ODIHR Election Observation Mission (EOM) report of campaign coverage in February and March 2002, state-funded television broadcaster UT-1 devoted between 21 percent and 40 percent of its prime-time presentations to the pro-presidential "For a United Ukraine" (FUU) political bloc of five parties, with most of the coverage being positive. Of the six large private television broadcasters, five still favored one political party or bloc over others, according to the EOM. The report stated that three broadcasters—Inter TV, Studio 1+1, and ICTV—provided more and favorable coverage of FUU and the SDPU(u)—Kuchma's party—whereas the smaller Utar and Noviy Canal (since taken over by pro-Kuchma interests) favored Viktor Yushchenko's "Our Ukraine" bloc and Yulia Tymoshenko. Inter TV and Studio 1+1 provided mostly negative reporting on Yushchenko and, just weeks before election day, ICTV—one of three broadcasters partially owned by the president's son-in-law Viktor Pinchuk—presented a controversial and inaccurate documentary connecting Western money to Ukraine's opposition. The program was rebroadcast on the state channel UT-1. Regional broadcasters owned by the state were deemed more biased, with channels in Kharkov and Nikolaiv dedicating some 70 percent of their news coverage to the pro-presidential FUU, which received only 11.77 percent of the vote.

While print media offered a greater plurality of political news coverage and views, readers still had to purchase several publications to see a balanced, complete picture of the campaign. In the 2002 elections, large-circulation daily newspapers *Fakty i Komentarii* (Facts and Commentary), *Segodnya* (Today), *Den* (Day) and *Kiyevskie Vedomosti* (The Kyiv Gazette) backed pro-presidential parties, while *Silski Visti* (Country News), *Ukraina Moloda* (The Youth of Ukraine) and *Vechernie Vesti* (The Evening Gazette) supported the opposition parties. The combined circulation of the national pro-government and government-controlled dailies exceeds 2.1 million, while the combined circulation of national dailies that are critical of the authorities stands at 1.15 million. Ukrainian editions of Russian periodicals, which have a combined national circulation of more than 700,000, tend to eschew criticism of the Kuchma administration. At the regional level, the imbalance is far greater, usually with a single local daily closely linked to the president-appointed regional governor or to pro-presidential local oligarchic groups.

The OSCE's EOM report also highlighted the politicized role of the Ukrainian Tax Administration, whose relentless investigations of independent media aroused a storm of domestic and international criticism. Although the tax administration temporarily froze investigations of news media organizations just before the 2002 elections, other forms of harassment surfaced. Several opposition newspapers had contracts cancelled by Kyiv printing houses, delaying and impeding publication. According to Professor Valeriy Ivanov, head of the mass media department at Kyiv National University, incidents in the regions included: a station's refusal to broadcast a program in which an opposition leader participated; publishing houses' refusing to print opposition periodicals; and distributors told not to sell several opposition newspapers. Professor Ivanov, who is also the head of the nongovernmental Academy of Ukrainian Press (AUP), noted further that the media frequently quoted biased public opinion polls that various political groupings had ordered, in an effort to disorient the electorate.

The same set of circumstances that ensured the media could not—or would not—play a constructive role as an independent and balanced participant before and during the last election prevails today. The media environment, in essence, has changed little over the past few years. Although there are several signs of increased civic monitoring and organized efforts by journalists to resist censorship and pressures, these are far too isolated to counterbalance the worrying state of affairs in the Ukrainian media scene.

Obstacles to Open and Fair Coverage

A range of interrelated factors contributes to Ukraine's troubling preelection news media environment. These include significant state interference and the economic dependency and vulnerability of most news media.

State Influence and Interference. State intimidation, state obstruction, and influence peddling as a means of personal economic gain continue to pull the strings that control many of Ukraine's news media. Most of the large-circulation national news publications in Kyiv are highly politicized— and most are tied to the incumbent government, to political parties, to oligarchic groupings known as financial-political groups, and to businessmen-parliamentarians. Media experts estimate that 90 percent of local and national newspapers and news magazines and 95 percent of television and radio stations are in the hands of political parties, national and local governments, or oligarchs and entrepreneurs influenced by or buddying with politicians. Television, the most popular medium in Ukraine, is also the most heavily controlled by government and politicians close to the ruling circles. At the national level, the only six major television broadcasters are controlled by the Kuchma regime or owned by Kuchma loyalists. STB—a station that bucked this trend in 1999—had its entire ownership team removed and replaced by allies of President Kuchma. Likewise, Novy Kanal, a station that gave voice to opposition parties in the 2002 elections, is under the control of a group closely connected to the president's son-in-law, Viktor Pinchuk.

State pressures on the media of Ukraine are hardly new. They were present in the first seriously contested Ukrainian election, the presidential race of 1994, when Kuchma unseated Leonid Kravchuk. At that time, local television media were harassed by the incumbent authorities. President Kuchma and, in recent years, his colleagues appear to have learned from the past and have applied the same tactics with a vengeance to political opponents.

The unfortunate result is that, after prospering and growing during the first days of Ukrainian independence, Ukraine's press freedoms in practice have gradually eroded. Notwithstanding the passage of a series of progressive media laws, today media freedoms are widely and systematically denied. Tax inspections, libel rulings against independent journalists, intimidation, state links to killings of journalists, questionable administrative controls over distribution, and revocation of broadcast licenses have stifled the operations of most independent news organizations and achieved alarming frequency and proportions in the 1999 presidential and 2002 parliamentary elections.

One disquieting and well-documented instance of direct state interference is the use of *temnyky*. Despite having been amply documented and revealed to the public during parliamentary committee hearings held late in 2002, *temnyky*—instructions from the presidential administration to news outlets directing the angle and substance of reporting a story— still exist today, although more discreetly. In a March 2003 study, "Negotiating the News: Informal State Censorship of Ukrainian Television," Human Rights Watch reported that *temnyky* were first sent to several pro-presidential news media companies and television stations in September 2001, during the campaigns prior to the March 2002 parliamentary elections. These directives have since been distributed to a larger number of broadcasters and are often reportedly followed up with intimidating phone calls from the presidential administration or by personal visits from enforcers. State-financed broadcasters and publications are required by the state to provide certain programming, which some editors and producers say forces them to cover stories from only one side or avoid certain topics. Otherwise, the news organizations risk loss of subsidies from governments—national, regional, or local.

Following protests and complaints by hundreds of journalists in October 2002 in Kyiv, the parliamentary Committee on Freedom of Speech and Information conducted hearings—during which the *temnyky* were brought to light—on political censorship and freedom-of-speech issues. From the meetings materialized a bill—signed into law by President Kuchma—that amended previous freedom-of-speech laws already in existence. The law is considered a significant positive step in Ukraine's development toward protecting press freedoms.

State interference is also severe at the local and regional levels, where officials (especially governors, who are appointed by the president and not by local elected councils) have grown more powerful over the years and have their own methods of harassing the print and broadcast media. In eastern Ukraine, journalists at several media outlets said they were not afraid to criticize "far-off" Kyiv but did express reservations about offending local and regional authorities. The editor-in-chief of one of the most popular newspapers in eastern Ukraine said his paper did not shy away from criticism but could only go so far—the local authorities owned the building where his paper was housed. Many editors find it easier to stick to social and cultural themes than to encourage sharp reporting that might risk pressure and official retaliation.

Blatant physical attacks against editors, producers, and reporters have continued since the 2000 murder of online reporter Georgy Gongadze. Among those who died under suspicious circumstances are Donetsky TV journalist Ihor Aleksandrov and Mykhaylo Kolomiytets, the head of the Ukrainian News Agency, who apparently committed suicide in November 2002. In other recent cases, online journalists Edouard Malinivsky (reporter with Ostriv) and Oleg Eltsov (editor of the Web site Ukraina Kryminalna) were assaulted by two thugs each in August and June 2003, respectively. Although direct connections have not been confirmed, the attacks have been investigated as retaliations for posted articles. Furthermore, the threat of violence has led some journalists to shy away from controversial political or economic topics. Almost half of 727 Ukrainian journalists polled in November 2002 by the Ukrainian Center of Economic and Political Research, the National Association of Journalists, Charter-4, and the Web-based media watchdog Telekritika believe physical retaliation from criminal elements or authorities is possible with the publication of critical materials. But psychological pressure (79.2 percent) and economic punishments (75.7 percent), the journalists said, are more frequent.

Economic Vulnerability. Although *temnyky* and attacks on journalists tend to garner much of the attention of international press-monitoring groups, many of the hurdles to attaining press freedom in Ukraine are neither criminal nor even strictly political in nature. Some stem from the financial weakness of Ukraine's media market.

Media magnates, businessmen, relatives of top government officials, and local administrators continue to abuse the news media to curry government favor and build power and influence. Owners of private media are known to pronounce editorial policies that support politicians and political parties, promote their own political aspirations, bury business competitors, and protect the interests of friends and family. As one interviewee put it, "In Ukraine, the way to make money is through politics and the way to do politics is through the media." One television news producer in a regional city said that political pressure was not the greatest impediment to independent journalism; the boss's attempts to please his business friends disturbed the producer much more. In this light, the government should be seen, said one journalism educator, as just one of several interest groups; it was unfair, he said, to blame President Kuchma alone for quashing press freedom.

In interviews conducted for this report, Kyiv-based national media professionals and rights monitors repeatedly highlighted the considerable degree of political interference and control exerted by the authorities or forces linked to them. By contrast, their counterparts at the local and regional levels—at least in the east, one of the main targets of this assessment—attribute their lack of independence far more to the economic climate. With a healthy advertising market and the other elements of a "normal" market economy, they believe their publications would be strong enough to resist both political forces and wealthy businessmen intending to use the press as a personal vehicle.

Ukraine's current advertising market—although it is growing by 30 percent annually—is very weak, especially for newspapers and news magazines. The situation is more robust in the capital, but about 75 to 80 percent of all ad revenues—which totaled between $80 million and $200 million last year according to various estimates—go to the six national television channels. These outlets, as noted above, are controlled by or support the current ruling administration. Jed Sunden, the publisher of the English-language *Kyiv Post* and the *Korrespondent* magazine and Web site, said newspapers take in only around 7 percent of ad revenue nationally, a very low figure compared to the more common 15 percent in other countries. He traced the situation to a number of factors, including a lack of skilled media managers and a dearth of Western investors—frightened off by the country's negative free-press image and the crash of the Russian ruble in 1998. At this point in the development of the market, Sunden said, newspaper executives should be able to take advantage of the rising economy, run their operations more efficiently, and devise innovative ways to increase circulation and attract more advertisers. Still, with the additional obstacle of a high proportion of Ukrainians living in poverty or possessing little discretionary disposable income, readership remains pitifully low, especially for a country of 48 million people.

Of the some 700 television and radio stations and 3,500 news publications on the market, about half admit to operating in the red. But it is suspected that actually most suffer losses. Those partially owned by or loyal to the Kuchma administration, regional governors, mayors, opposition leaders, and political parties are kept financially afloat by government subsidies and/or hidden handouts. Lack of transparency, submission of false data to the National Council, and hidden ownership make it increasingly difficult to know the financial truth.

Some of the journalists and editors interviewed for this report felt the fastest way to a genuine media market would be for the state to relinquish its ownership and stop the practice of subsidies as quickly as possible. As a result, unappealing, politicized newspapers and broadcasters would, they say, disappear from the scene. The privatization of state-owned media would, this theory goes, boost the demand for Western-style journalism, allowing journalists to pursue freedom of speech and recast news media as real businesses. Others, however, worried that media oligarchs would snatch up newly freed news organizations, and the currently enforced editorial policies would continue as they do today. "Privatization under the current market conditions is horrifying," said Sergiy Guz, the general secretary of the Kyiv Independent Media Union, predicting greater economic pressure on journalists and continued political control of publications and broadcasters.

Events since January 2004

While media repression has long been a calling card of President Leonid Kuchma's regime, the year 2004 has unleashed a new, and in some ways unprecedented, campaign against Ukraine's independent and opposition media. Through intimidation and direct intervention, the authorities have targeted all types of media, from broadcasters to the press to the Internet. Although concerned about the developments, both the international community and Ukrainian civil society have been largely powerless to counter the wide range of tactics employed by the presidential administration and its allies.

Non–state-controlled radio has been particularly hard hit; the shutdowns of stations were so extensive that press-rights groups and Western governments pointed to a concerted attempt to remove alternative voices and political debate from the airwaves. The first closure occurred in January, when the local health authorities turned off Radio Rox, an opposition-friendly station whose live broadcasts from parliament included speeches by opposition members. Rox had also aired news programs from independent Public Radio, a station that otherwise operates only on the Internet, as the authorities have not granted it a frequency. Radio Rox returned to the air in April, at which point it continued to broadcast from parliament but ceased Public Radio programming.

In February, Radio Free Europe/Radio Liberty disappeared from FM after the new head of Radio Dovira, which had broadcast RFE/RL programs for five years, ended the agreement, saying Dovira would now be focusing on entertainment shows. Critics saw a political connection, as the new director is known as a Kuchma loyalist.

In response to Dovira's move, on February 27 Serhiy Sholokh, director of Kyiv's Radio Kontynent, began airing a two-hour rebroadcast of RFE/RL on his station. Kontynent was already on the authorities' blacklist for carrying the programs of the BBC Ukrainian Service, Deutsche Welle, and the Voice of America, and the RFE/RL arrangement was short-lived. On March 3, police seized Kontynent's transmitter and sealed its offices, citing the expiration of the station's FM broadcast license. The license, however, had in fact run out in 2001, thus prompting doubts over the timing of the current raid. Sholokh subsequently fled the country, saying people connected to the United Social Democratic Party of presidential chief of staff Viktor Medvedchuk had threatened him.

Press defense organizations have also raised questions over the death of Heorhiy Chechyk, director of the private radio and television company Yuta, which owns FM Radio Poltava Plus. On March 3, Chechyk was on his way to a meeting with local executives of RFE/RL when his car hit another vehicle. The police have ruled Chechyk's death an accident. Others, however, have demanded a full investigation, citing a long line of suspicious automobile accidents involving opposition politicians and supporters. Moreover, a number of other radio stations that were in negotiations with RFE/RL at the time of Chechyk's death subsequently backed out for fear of prosecution.

Moves against television stations were not as prevalent as those involving radio, although that is probably because nearly all channels are already in the hands of those either close to the regime or sufficiently intimidated so as not to offer alternative news programming. The sole remaining pro-opposition station, Channel 5, owned by a supporter of leading opposition candidate Viktor Yushchenko, debuted in the summer of 2003. However, it may be on its last legs, as another station has sued it in an attempt to acquire its broadcasting frequency.

In addition to the above attacks, which have generated a good bit of attention abroad, actions that received less notice have been taken against smaller regional broadcasters, such as M-Studio. This television channel was the most popular in the Transcarpathian region, but the authorities took it off the air in the run-up to the disputed April 18 mayoral election in the station's hometown, Mukacheve. By many accounts, that election was blatantly rigged in favor of the government candidate. On the brighter side, a few smaller stations, such as ICTV, STB, and Novyi Kanal, have begun airing more diverse coverage, perhaps because their owners are hedging their political bets.

The press has not escaped unscathed, either. In January, a court in Kyiv ordered the closure of *Silski Visti*, one of the largest-selling national dailies, which is close to the opposition Socialist Party. The paper had broken a law concerning the publication of extremist views (in this case, paid anti-Semitic advertising). Critics have charged, however, that the court acted selectively, as both the author and other anti-Semitic publications have escaped punishment. One Jewish figure—Yevhen Chervonenko, vice president of the Eurasian Jewish Congress (and an aide to Yushchenko)—labeled the move a "calculated provocation by the presidential administration against the media." *Silski Visti* appealed the decision; in all likelihood, the lengthy court process will now last until after the presidential elections, allowing the paper to continue to appear.

Filling a crucial gap in coverage, Internet media continue to thrive, serving as one of the only sources of independent, hard-hitting news and analysis. Growth in the number of Internet users continues to explode, although estimates about the percentage of the population with access continue to vary dramatically, from 6 percent to a more likely 12 to 15 percent. In addition, a Freedom House Kyiv survey released in May 2004 indicated that only 0.2 percent of the population consider the Internet their primary source of information. Nearly 73 percent mentioned national television as their main source, 7 percent cited radio, and 10 percent newspapers. However, the low figure for the Internet is somewhat misleading as many regional newspapers, particularly small ones, republish Internet news and information.

Some analysts believe that the government may scale back the relative freedom on the Internet as election day approaches, using new legislation to suppress unfriendly sites. Late in 2003, President Kuchma signed into law a restrictive bill passed by parliament in November, mandating that Internet service providers (ISPs) install and maintain monitoring equipment at their own expense. Government agencies—such as the Secret Service of Ukraine (SBU), the successor to the KGB—may then use this equipment to tap private electronic communication, a nightmare for enterprising (and investigative) journalists. An even more intimidating piece of legislation, the Law on Activities in the Area of Information Technology, stalled after passing its first reading in November. That draft law, which appears to have gone too far even for some government-connected parliamentary deputies, mandated that ISPs and users transmit only "true, complete, and timely information" and contained vaguely worded bans on distributing libelous or distorted information.

Intimidation has also been used against Internet groups. On January 12, 2004, unknown assailants fired rubber bullets at the editor-in-chief of the Ukraina Kriminalnaya Web site, which has published articles exposing the illicit activities of the government elite. In May, Olexandre Pomytkin, a journalist for the site, was arrested and charged with fraud; his colleagues attribute the allegation to his recent book on connections between the mafia and police. Kostyantyn Sydorenko—a journalist covering the Mukacheve mayoral election for www.hotline.com.ua, an election-monitoring website—was arrested on May 22, 2004. He was then quickly sentenced to five days in prison for resisting the security forces, although his real crime may have been taking sensitive footage of the police removing a group of activists. "We do question the real reasons for their arrests," said Reporters Without Borders in a statement. "It is all the more important to look into these cases because both of them were investigating issues that are sensitive for the authorities."

In addition, the leading opposition Web site, Ukrayinska Pravda, and the opposition daily, *Ukrayina Moloda,* were sued for libel this spring by two people who are believed to be Medvedchuk's proxies. The two demand that the assets of the two media groups be frozen pending the hearing.

The authorities have responded to the criticisms over meddling in the media, but most analysts doubt the sincerity of their actions. The television stations owned by Viktor Pinchuk, the president's son-in-law, have been providing more coverage—though still limited—of opposition voices. Pinchuk has also renounced his membership in the pro-Kuchma Working Ukraine party and partnered with George Soros to establish a joint legal aid foundation. While some see these moves as an attempt to carve out more moderate territory in case Yushchenko wins, others view the actions as camouflage to impress the international community while the status quo remains the same behind the scenes. Similarly, few believed Prime Minister Viktor Yanukovich's May 6, 2004, speech defending the rights of the media.

Whether these actions against the media will prompt significant opposition at home or abroad is an open question. Western governments have condemned the crackdown and issued increasingly overt warnings, including resolutions in both houses of the U.S. Congress, about the need for a democratic, transparent, and fair election process. However, those threats, which will almost certainly increase as election day approaches, are unlikely to help mobilize the Ukrainian public, as they probably will not make it further than the small opposition press and independent Web sites. According to the opposition Web site Ukrayinska Pravda, the presidential administration has issued a series of *temnyky* forbidding any reporting on negative statements by international organizations or governments. Combined with moves to force RFE/RL and other Western-backed news services off the air, this suggests a determined attempt to shield the electorate from criticism emanating from Brussels and Washington. Such an attempt would serve the ruling party well, as most voters favor European integration and their exposure to harsh words that continually put that goal in doubt could spell trouble for government-supported candidates in the presidential election and further damage the regime's popularity overall.

At the beginning of March 2004, when roughly 5,000 Ukrainians did take to the streets of Kyiv, media shutdowns were one of the major themes of the antigovernment protest. However, the demonstrations have not developed into a cause with any momentum. It is likely that the country's burgeoning civil society—including more than 100 NGOs that have united to form a civic coalition called New Choice 2004—will have to rally support for free media and offer unbiased election information to the population. All signs currently indicate the inability of the media to perform either function, with intimidation from the authorities the chief cause.

In Defiance of Common Sense: The Practical Effects of International Press Restrictions

Ronald Koven

"There are no principles contained in the Universal Declaration of Human Rights," said the chief Chinese delegate to the assembled representatives of the countries in the UN system. This statement, made at one of the last preparatory conferences for the World Summit on the Information Society, was intended to justify his refusal to go along with a new declaration that any "information society" should be based on the principles of the Universal Declaration. Paradoxically, the Chinese assertion was so breathtakingly absurd that it underlined the importance that China attaches to the adoption of international texts that legitimize—or at least that do not delegitimize—its repressive practices.

One might as well ask whether statements by international organizations, in and out of the UN system, on issues related to press freedom have any practical effects on the everyday activities of the news media in print, broadcast, and now the Internet? Common sense might suggest that public statements and word choices have insignificant impact on real life practices. We must keep reminding ourselves that this is simply not the case. It may indeed be true that some of the worst offenders against press freedom— such as Belarus, Burma, and Zimbabwe—do not care what the international community says, since they will continue to control the press regardless. But other authoritarian countries—led by China, Cuba, and Vietnam and

---

Ronald Koven is the European Representative of the World Press Freedom Committee, and has held major editing and/or reporting positions at the International Herald Tribune, Washington Post and Boston Globe. He was a participant in the preparatory conferences for the World Summit on the Information Society.

joined at various times by a great variety of states such as Russia, Venezuela, Pakistan, Malaysia, Egypt, and Syria—spend enormous amounts of time and energy attempting to persuade the international community to adopt texts and measures that would justify the restrictions they place on free speech, press freedom, and other human rights.

The World Summit on the Information Society

A recent example was the UN's December 2003 World Summit on the Information Society (WSIS) in Geneva, which was the culmination of two years of preparatory meetings. The negotiations were an excruciating exercise in damage control, but in the end, press-freedom groups were largely successful in averting notable backsliding. This was in part because Switzerland, the host country, is firmly attached to press freedom. The Swiss worked hard with press-freedom groups to help forestall some of the most damaging proposals so that their country's name would not be associated with regression on press freedom. For instance, the Swiss president made a last-minute trip to Beijing just before the actual summit to appeal to Chinese leaders.

Still, a follow-up summit will be held at the end of 2005 in Tunisia, a country that holds hundreds of political prisoners and regularly jails journalists for offenses such as disrespect for state institutions. Tunisia's is one of the world's cleverest regimes at creating a positive image for itself abroad. During the Geneva summit, the Tunisians confiscated copies of the summit newspaper, *Terra Viva* (published by the Third-World activist Inter Press Service), because it contained comments critical of Tunisia's highly repressive free-speech/press-freedom record. Tunisian "truth squads" intervened, often very boisterously, at virtually every preparatory committee meeting where there was even mild criticism of their country.

For their part, the Chinese made it known that they would compromise on their restrictionist stance provided that the summit accepted language authorizing the Chinese to control Internet traffic inside their country. This would have legitimized Chinanet, the Internet Service Provider system already in place. It acts as an Intranet instead of an Internet, preventing "undesirable" exchanges with the outside world. Internally, it monitors communications to detect deviant sentiments. Unlike countries that dress up their controls with appeals to positive-sounding objectives like protecting morality, promoting social harmony, economic development, and so forth, China has been frank to admit that it seeks political control—or "information sovereignty," as the Chinese call it.

In the two years leading up to the second World Summit on the Information Society in Tunis, governments will be lobbying to end the current system of strictly neutral rule-keeping for the Internet, which today is maintained by a technical, California-based corporation. In its place, countries as disparate as China and a number of West European democracies seek oversight by an intergovernmental body, with authority over content and ethics. Granting content controls even to "friendly" governments like France and Germany, not to speak of China and Cuba, would inevitably lead to the end of press freedom on the Internet.

Some governments argued in Geneva for a new "Right to Communicate" in the final summit. They said this would improve upon the established press-freedom guarantees of Article 19 of the Universal Declaration of Human Rights. The "Right to Communicate" first surfaced in the 1980s as part of the controversial "New World Information and Communication Order"—an attempt by the Soviets and Third-World authoritarians to introduce a large variety of international press controls. While it has taken many ill-defined forms, one constant of the "Right to Communicate" has been that it provides governments and groups the right to space and air time in other people's news media for "equitable" presentations of their views, taking away the freedom of the editors to decide what to run. Radical groups active at the first summit have indicated that they will continue their efforts to establish such a "Right to Communicate" in the future.

Justifying the Controls

The countries that seek international blessings for domestic controls are not only the usual suspects still in thrall to Communism or post-colonial authoritarianism. Some are allies of the West. Many quietly allow others to carry the ball for repression while they watch attentively for openings they can use to justify their own press-freedom restrictions. The "Stans"—the newly independent republics of Central Asia—are particularly adept at this approach. Even countries joining Western institutions such as the European Union, the Council of Europe, and NATO use such tactics. Such countries invoke standards contained in the laws of established democracies or in international laws and conventions to justify fining or jailing journalists and/or restricting or even closing down their news media outlets. For instance:

∎ Romania claims that a particularly broad and repressive state secrets law it has been considering is designed to meet NATO requirements.

∎ Bulgaria's supreme court ruled that insult laws giving special protection to the state's leaders simply followed models on the books throughout Western Europe, failing to note that those laws are considered anachronistic in the West.

∎ Turkey regularly justifies the jailing of Kurdish journalists and commentators by citing the European Human Rights Convention's Article 10, which allows for restrictions on freedom of expression to maintain the "territorial integrity" of member states.

Moreover, the international community has often set poor examples with questionable actions against news media in countries and territories under international control, as in Bosnia, Kosovo, and Iraq.

Would-be press controllers also justify their actions by exploiting the words of those speaking in the name of the UN and other international bodies. After a recent visit to the Ivory Coast, the UN Human Rights Commission's newly named Special Rapporteur on the Right to Freedom of Opinion and Expression, Ambeyi Ligabo, attributed the very real problems of the press in a country prey to civil war to "the lack of regulatory mechanisms which entail obligations, responsibility and discipline amongst newspaper publishers and editors." Such emphasis on media accountability, however well meant, is easily exploited by repressive regimes.

Media Restrictions by Established Democracies and International Institutions

Ligabo is not the only international official appointed to promote press freedom who wound up calling for restrictive measures. The first major public act of the newly appointed Representative on Freedom of the Media of the Organization for Security and Cooperation in Europe, Miklos Haraszti, was to issue a report in spring 2004 calling for severe new restrictions on news media in Kosovo. The report was a response to alleged incitement to intercommunal violence by news coverage of an incident in which three Albanian boys drowned in a river while fleeing Serbian taunters. Among other things, the OSCE report said, "In journalistic terms even the incident as such is not a *fact* until the respective authorities have confirmed it [italics original]."

In like manner, the Committee of Ministers of the Council of Europe issued a "Declaration on Freedom of Political Debate in the Media" in February 2004 that took the position that political figures and public officials have the same rights of privacy as private persons. That statement flies in the face of the opinions of leading judicial bodies such as the Inter American Human Rights Commission, the U.S. Supreme Court, and Europe's own Court of Human Rights that the press must be free to scrutinize public figures more than purely private persons. So strong was the reflexive desire of members of the committee of ministers to avoid public scrutiny that the ministerial statement was adopted even after the ministers were advised by their own international law experts that it would be a step backward for press freedom.

Moreover, established democracies such as France, Italy, and Spain successfully pressured the Council of Europe to allow for the protection of governmental institutions, in addition to individuals, from defamation. Legal justifications were offered based on Italian and Spanish texts promulgated under Mussolini and Franco. In defiance of a UN Human Rights Commission statement that prison terms should never be imposed for expressions of opinion, the ministers said that incarceration would be acceptable as a "strictly necessary and proportionate penalty" for "defamation or insult by the media." The Council of Europe has also insisted on issuing rules against "illegal and harmful content" in the news media. The vague and subjective notion of "harmful content" was adopted despite warnings from a number of distinguished lawyers of the dangers of abuse of such overly broad language.

Meanwhile, the Parliamentary Assembly of the European Union has been seriously considering a bill subjecting Internet publishers to defamation actions in any country where contested material is downloaded. It would mean that media outlets that publish on the Internet would need to protect themselves against the often widely differing laws of other European Union countries, an endeavor that would be so burdensome as to have a major chilling effect on reporting and comment on other countries. The bill could also potentially be used to extend criminal defamation laws beyond a country's own borders, even if they are in clear violation of accepted world press-freedom standards.

Just such an outcome came about in Australia, where the Supreme Court ruled in December 2002 that *Barron's* weekly of New York is liable under the defamation laws of Australia's Victoria State—literally on the other side of the globe—for an article about an Australian businessman. *Barron's* has next to no circulation in Australia, but the court held that the suit was valid given that someone in Victoria could have consulted the weekly's Web site.

Recently, the Russian news agency TASS called for the creation of a "World Council of News Agencies" in Moscow in fall 2004. TASS received support for the initiative from leaders of the UN and UNESCO as a contribution to promoting a "pluralistic information society" and "equitable access to free and independent information." Given that TASS's devotion to its government's official line has not changed notably since it served as a leading Soviet propaganda organ, such a UN-endorsed council is unlikely to help create pluralistic, free, or independent information.

In Iraq, the U.S.-led Coalition Provisional Authority imposed a 60-day ban of a weekly newspaper backing the violently rebellious cleric Muqtada Al-Sadr in March 2004. The weekly, *Al Hawza,* was accused of inciting violence by reporting an allegation that some 50 Iraqi police cadets were killed not by a terrorist car bomb but by a rocket fired from a U.S. helicopter. Another reproach by the CPA was that the paper had compared CPA chief Paul Bremer to the deposed dictator Saddam Hussein.

The ban was presented as part of the strategy to curb the violence that has followed the spring 2003 invasion. The ban not only contradicted the democratic principles the Coalition claims it is trying to bring to Iraq. It also touched off even more violence. Furthermore, authoritarian regimes are likely to see the ban as an example that justifies their own press controls.

The Role of Press-Freedom Advocates

Press-freedom groups such as the World Press Freedom Committee have waged many battles in the international arena. They played a major role in turning UNESCO into a champion of press freedom, even if vigilance is needed against occasional, mostly inadvertent backsliding. Press-freedom groups also worked to persuade U.S. officials not to allow security concerns after September 11, 2001, to supercede traditional U.S.

support in international organizations for press-freedom concerns. In addition, these groups have turned the tide against the advance of "insult laws," which give special protection to governments and their officials; moves to abrogate such laws have been seen in countries as widely separated as Chile, Costa Rica, Ghana, and Norway.

Yet, no victory is ever final, and those seeking to restrict the media (often lurking in surprising places) are constantly on the lookout for new or updated ways to do so. So, press freedom groups must continue their work in defense of the public's right to freedom of the press as a fundamental part of democracy.

COUNTRY REPORTS AND RATINGS

Afghanistan

Status: Not Free

LEGAL ENVIRONMENT: 24
POLITICAL ENVIRONMENT: 28
ECONOMIC ENVIRONMENT: 20
TOTAL SCORE: 72

Although conditions for Afghanistan's media have improved markedly since the fall of the repressive Taliban regime in late 2001, journalists remained subject to a range of legal and political pressures in 2003. A press law adopted in February 2002 guarantees the right to freedom of expression but also contains a number of broadly worded restrictions on licensing and foreign ownership, as well as insult laws that could be subject to abuse. In June 2003, two editors of the Kabul-based newspaper *Aftab* were arrested briefly and charged with blasphemy, and in July the fatwa (religious edict) department of the Supreme Court recommended that they be sentenced to death; the case was pending at year's end. Authorities have granted more than 200 licenses to private publications and have begun licensing a number of private radio stations and cable television operators. However, cable television services were banned by the conservative chief justice of the Supreme Court in January; they resumed only in April after the government drew up a broadcasting code and a list of authorized stations and permissible content. National and local governments continue to own or control several dozen newspapers and almost all of the electronic media. On the other hand, access to the Internet and to international radio broadcasts, on which many Afghans rely for information, is largely unrestricted. Media diversity remains most pronounced in Kabul, as some regional warlords have refused to allow independent media outlets to operate in the areas under their control. During 2003, a number of journalists were harassed or violently attacked by security services, government ministers, military leaders, and others in positions of power as a result of their reporting. Zahur Afghan, the editor of the *Erada* daily, received numerous death threats in April after publishing an article that was critical of the education ministry, and another prominent journalist who spoke out against local warlords was attacked and stabbed by an unidentified assailant later that month. In Herat, a correspondent for Radio Free Europe/Radio Liberty was beaten, jailed, and then expelled from the region by security forces loyal to local governor and strongman Ismail Khan. As a result, many journalists practice self-censorship or avoid writing about sensitive issues such as Islam, national unity, or crimes committed by specific warlords. In the country's underdeveloped economic environment, the majority of media outlets remain dependent on the state, political parties, or international donors for financial support.

Albania

Status: Partly Free

LEGAL ENVIRONMENT: 17
POLITICAL ENVIRONMENT: 18
ECONOMIC ENVIRONMENT: 14
TOTAL SCORE: 49

Although the constitution provides for freedom of expression, political interference in the media remains a serious problem. The majority of media outlets are affiliated with a political party; public television continues to function as a medium for government propaganda, regardless of the political party in power. Legislation was passed in 2003 requiring balanced party representation on public television's board of directors. Nevertheless, the opposition asserts that the majority of board members are closely aligned with the ruling party. There are more than 200 newspapers, some 50 TV stations, and 30 radio stations; as with other countries in the region, television serves as the primary source of information for the average Albanian. According to the OSCE office in Albania, some 60 percent of media advertising is paid for by budget-financed or state institutions. The government is known to grant state advertising to those media providing favorable coverage. Furthermore, private businesses are increasingly wary of advertising with antigovernment media groups lest they risk financial audits. Private broadcasters also suffer burdensome state levies, including licensing fees and other taxes. In July, the government blocked broadcasting by one of the largest networks in the country, ALSAT TV, for reportedly failing to pay taxes and other fees. The station asserts that the government acted for political reasons, but at year's end it was able to operate only sporadically. A decree prohibits senior civil servants from providing any official information to the media, although the prime minister privately revoked this decree just five days before the Constitutional Court was due to consider its legality. Journalists are paid poorly, which makes them susceptible to corruption. On several occasions, government officials have been linked to threats against journalists.

LEGAL ENVIRONMENT: 23
POLITICAL ENVIRONMENT: 22

Algeria
ECONOMIC ENVIRONMENT: 18

Status: Not Free
TOTAL SCORE: 63

Although Algeria's private press is among the most vibrant in the region, press freedom here suffered alarming setbacks in 2003. As pre-election tension rose, the government imposed new constraints on freedom of expression and began a campaign of intimidation, legal harassment, and financial pressure on the independent media. The State of Emergency Law (in effect since 1992) and the restrictive 2001 penal code amendments undermine constitutional provisions for freedom of speech and give the government authority to impose harsh fines and jail sentences for cases in which journalists "defame, insult or injure" government officials or institutions. In August 2003, six independent newspapers were suspended (*Le Matin, Le Soir d'Algerie, Liberte, L'Expression, El Khabar, and Errai*), and their journalists, editors, and publishers arrested on charges of defamation. However, by the end of the year all had been released from jail without charge. Notably, for the first time in years, the independent press reported on formerly taboo topics such as government wiretaps, corruption, and human rights violations in Kabylie. However, coverage of these and other controversial issues—Islam, the courts, and the military—is still minimal due to journalists' limited access to information and broad-scale self-censorship. Foreign media were prohibited from covering the release from jail of two key leaders of the banned Islamic Salvation Front (FIS). Furthermore, the state continued to exert control over independent media content through its distribution of advertising on political grounds and its virtual monopoly of the nation's printing presses. Although a 1998 amendment to the information code provides for private broadcast ownership, the Algerian government maintains total control over national television and radio. Coverage remains biased in favor of government policies, but foreign programming is easily accessible through widely available satellite dishes and antennae. Since 2001, no censorship of the Internet has been reported. However, only a small percentage of Algerians use the Internet, and only the government can grant licenses to Internet service providers.

Andorra

LEGAL ENVIRONMENT: 1
POLITICAL ENVIRONMENT: 4
ECONOMIC ENVIRONMENT: 8

Status: Free

TOTAL SCORE: 13

The first Andorran constitution, ratified in 1993, provides for freedom of speech and of the press. Media outlets operate freely. The legal system provides for the right to reply in cases of slander. The media scene is shaped by the country's proximity to France and Spain, as Andorrans have access to broadcasts from both countries. There are three radio stations and two major dailies: *Diari d'Andorra* and *El Periodic*. The primary TV station is TVA, operated by Radio i Television d'Andorra. Independent media are active and express a wide variety of views, including those critical of the government.

Angola

LEGAL ENVIRONMENT: 18
POLITICAL ENVIRONMENT: 27
ECONOMIC ENVIRONMENT: 21

Status: Not Free

TOTAL SCORE: 66

Conditions for the media continued to improve in 2003 as the consolidation of peace progressed following the signing of an accord between the government and rebel fighters in 2002. Although the constitution states that the media cannot be subjected to censorship, the government does not always respect this provision in practice. Defamation of the president or his representatives is a criminal offense for which there is no truth defense; it is punishable by imprisonment or fines. In January, the government threatened legal action against the privately owned weekly *Angolense*, citing the magazine's publication of several articles accusing 59 top government figures of corruption and embezzlement. Reporters continue to face various forms of official harassment, including the confiscation of travel documents and limitations on the right to travel. However, incidents of arbitrary arrest, detention, physical attacks, and other tactics of severe government repression have decreased substantially in the postwar period. Although some journalists practice self-censorship when reporting on sensitive issues, the private print and broadcast media are generally free to scrutinize government policies. State-owned outlets, including the only television station, dominate the Angolan media and favor the ruling party. However, in 2003 the government announced plans to open the television sector to privately owned broadcasters. In the recent past, the government has reportedly paid journalists to publish complimentary stories and has discouraged advertisers from buying space in independent newspapers, thus threatening their financial viability.

Antigua and Barbuda

LEGAL ENVIRONMENT: 12
POLITICAL ENVIRONMENT: 16
ECONOMIC ENVIRONMENT: 15

Status: Partly Free

TOTAL SCORE: 43

The constitution provides for freedom of expression. However, the dominant Antigua Labour Party (ALP) and the Bird family continue to hinder equal access to opposition parties through broadcast and print media. Local free-press advocates have called for reform of existing media laws, arguing that current laws prohibit critical public discussion. The government and members of the ruling party own or control most broadcast outlets. Despite previous promises that the state-owned media would be privatized, in 2003 there was no major change in media holdings. Some corporations reportedly do not advertise on the only independent radio station for fear of losing government contracts. With legislative elections scheduled for 2004, the Electoral Commission met with several media houses to discuss regulations managing the conduct of broadcast and print media in the run-up to the polling. Current laws require that the media provide "equitable allocation of time and space, in a non-discriminatory manner to enable political parties and candidates to carry their messages." However, the chief information officer of the state-owned media suggested that parties be allotted proportional time based on their seat distribution in parliament, which was interpreted by some as conflicting with already agreed-to laws that all political parties be afforded equal time on the state-owned media.

LEGAL ENVIRONMENT: 8
POLITICAL ENVIRONMENT: 14

Argentina
ECONOMIC ENVIRONMENT: 13

Status: Partly Free
TOTAL SCORE: 35

A degree of stability has returned in Argentina after the political and economic turmoil of 2002. As a result of this slow return to normality, the ability of the press to operate freely has also increased. Though Argentina's constitution provides for a free and independent press, and though the country's press has traditionally been vibrant and freely critical of the government, reporters allege that the government tries to control viewpoints in the media through its allocation of advertising revenue. In the run-up to presidential elections held in April 2003, rival supporters of each candidate— the challenger, Nestor Kirchner, who was elected, and the incumbent Carlos Menem, who was defeated—attacked cameramen and other reporters documenting the mob-like behavior and intimidation of innocent bystanders occurring at political rallies. Since Kirchner assumed power in May 2003, attacks on the press have abated somewhat, but journalists, particularly those who report on corruption and other sensitive issues, are still subjected to threats and physical violence at the hands of the police and other actors. President Kirchner's government has pushed for a series of anticorruption measures and progressive reforms in the legislature, including a set of laws establishing transparency in, free reporting of, and public access to legislative and judicial proceedings. Passage of these laws is contingent on Senate approval. Nevertheless, libel remains a criminal offense and is sometimes used to prosecute journalists. Fiscal pressures created by Argentina's stagnating economy have also offset these positive political developments. Drops in circulation and advertising have threatened the economic viability of private media outlets, which continue to fold in record numbers. In December, in an effort to correct this situation, the legislature revoked a value-added tax on advertising revenue that had been disproportionately affecting small and medium-size press outlets.

Legal Environment: 20
Political Environment: 26
Economic Environment: 18

Armenia

Status: Not Free

Total Score: 64

Despite constitutional guarantees for freedom of speech and the press, these rights are limited in practice. Journalists practice self-censorship, particularly in reporting on issues of national security and government corruption. In December 2003, a draft media law was adopted that requires media outlets to reveal their sources in closed hearings if the subjects of their reports are determined to relate to national security. The authorities frequently use criminal defamation and insult laws against journalists critical of the government, and a new criminal code adopted in April did not repeal articles criminalizing defamation. In a positive step, parliament passed a new Freedom of Information Law in September that requires various state agencies and some private organizations to release requested information to the public in a timely manner. The leading independent television station, A1+, which lost its license in a controversial 2002 broadcasting frequency tender, had subsequent efforts to renew its license in 2003 rejected by a regulatory body whose members were appointed by President Robert Kocharian. The decision was widely believed to be politically motivated, as A1+ frequently aired coverage critical of the government. Several independent journalists faced harassment and physical assaults during the run-up to the 2003 national elections and while investigating corruption by state officials. The state-owned television channel is heavily influenced by the government, while the leading private television stations are also largely pro-Kocharian. Armenia's private newspapers offer more diverse opinions than the broadcast media. However, the country's difficult economic climate, combined with low circulation levels, leaves them financially dependent on business or political interest groups who exercise de facto editorial control over content.

Australia

Legal Environment: 3
Political Environment: 4
Economic Environment: 7

Status: Free
Total Score: 14

The government respects freedom of the press and speech, even though the constitution does not specifically provide for these rights. Citizens and media frequently criticize the government without reprisal. A vibrant independent media exists; privately owned TV and radio provide most information. However, Australia's media ownership is considered to be highly concentrated, and current concern rests on re-introduced amendments to cross-ownership laws that would further relax limitations on ownership. Currently, the Murdoch-owned News Corporation controls about 70 percent of urban newspapers while the Fairfax group controls the remaining 30 percent.

Austria

Legal Environment: 9
Political Environment: 8
Economic Environment: 6

Status: Free
Total Score: 23

Austria remained a free media environment in 2003. The federal constitution and the Media Law of 1981 provide the basis for a free press. Seldom-used legal restrictions, which forbid reporting deemed detrimental to morality or national security, remain. Observers, including the European Court of Human Rights, complain about the use of libel and slander laws to shelter politicians and other government officials and the impact these laws have on coverage. Media concentration is a concern as a conglomerate of the two largest publishing groups, Newsgroup and Mediaprint, controls 60 percent of the daily newspaper market and nearly 100 percent of the magazine market. The Austrian Broadcasting Corporation (ORF) continues to dominate both the radio and television markets. However, a variety of private radio stations exists, and laws passed in 2002 permit private television stations. In June 2003, ATV Plus, the first private TV channel, was available nationwide. Internet access is unrestricted and widely available.

Azerbaijan

Status: Not Free

LEGAL ENVIRONMENT: 24
POLITICAL ENVIRONMENT: 26
ECONOMIC ENVIRONMENT: 21
TOTAL SCORE: 71

Although the constitution and media laws guarantee freedom of speech and the press, the government restricts these rights in practice and self-censorship is common. Libel is a criminal offense, and dozens of defamation lawsuits were filed during 2003 against independent journalists and newspapers who criticized the government and reported on corruption. Among those targeted were *Yeni Musavat*, a newspaper associated with the opposition Musavat party, and Elmar Huseynov, editor-in-chief of the *Monitor* magazine. The judiciary, which is not independent of the executive branch and is widely believed to be corrupt and inefficient, rarely renders impartial verdicts in cases concerning the media. During the weeks before and after the October 2003 presidential election, journalists suffered increased intimidation, detention, and attacks, including physical assaults while reporting on political opposition rallies. *Yeni Musavat* editor Rauf Arifoglu was sentenced to three months in prison for allegedly organizing public demonstrations immediately following the election. State and private television stations are under the control or influence of the government. The members of the National Television and Radio Council, which licenses and regulates broadcasters, are appointed by the president. Although the press enjoys greater freedom than the broadcast media, state-funded papers reflect the ruling party's position on various issues, and private print media often have ties to and serve the agendas of opposition parties. In 2003, a number of opposition papers were denied access to the state-run printing and distribution system. Most newspapers are printed in government publishing houses, which periodically have refused to print independent or opposition papers with unpaid debts. In January, President Heydar Aliev froze the print media's debts to the state publishing house through 2005. The country's economic problems limit the ability of independent newspapers to survive through newsstand sales, and government pressure on businesses restricts advertising in opposition publications.

Bahamas

Status: Free

LEGAL ENVIRONMENT: 4
POLITICAL ENVIRONMENT: 5
ECONOMIC ENVIRONMENT: 5
TOTAL SCORE: 14

The Bahamas continue to enjoy a free press, which is guaranteed by the constitution. Numerous privately owned radio stations and newspapers provide a broad array of political views and can openly criticize the government and its policies. The state-owned Broadcasting Corporation of the Bahamas is the country's only television station. It is generally said to be free of government influence, though it has been criticized as offering preferential coverage to the ruling party. Media laws have been amended to allow for private ownership of broadcasting outlets, and there is unrestricted access to the Internet. Strict libel laws are currently on the books; nevertheless, journalists generally perform their job unhindered. Citizens are watching closely to see what the recently appointed Constitutional Commission will recommend with respect to freedom of speech. It is hoped that the government will embrace the opportunity to replace some of the more restrictive slander and defamation laws with modern libel laws. Local media reports indicate that Foreign Minister Fred Mitchell, a former journalist, is supportive of eliminating these archaic laws.

Bahrain

Status: Not Free

LEGAL ENVIRONMENT: 22
POLITICAL ENVIRONMENT: 25
ECONOMIC ENVIRONMENT: 23
TOTAL SCORE: 70

The constitution allows for the right to press freedom, excluding opinions that undermine the fundamental beliefs of Islam or the "unity of the people" and those that promote "discord or sectarianism." In practice, the government significantly restricts this right. While criticism in the press of government policies and the expression of opinions on domestic and foreign issues has increased in recent years, the 2002 Press Law includes 17 categories of offenses, 3 of which allow for prison sentences. Despite the fact that the prime minister declared the Press Law to be "frozen" one week after its issuance, the government continues to enforce it at its discretion. Most notably, in March 2003 authorities sentenced Manour Al Jamry, the editor-in-chief of the only truly independent newspaper, *Al-Wasat*, to one month in jail or a large fine (his case is on appeal) for publishing sensitive information concerning a local terrorist cell. Another *Al-Wasat* employee involved in this matter was fined as well. The government owns and operates all radio and television stations in the country, and these outlets broadcast only official views. Print media are privately owned, but they usually exercise self-censorship in articles covering sensitive topics. Broadcast media from neighboring countries are available, though the government continues to ban the Qatar-based news channel Al-Jazeera. The government remains the country's only Internet provider.

Bangladesh
Status: Not Free

LEGAL ENVIRONMENT: 19
POLITICAL ENVIRONMENT: 31
ECONOMIC ENVIRONMENT: 18
TOTAL SCORE: 68

The Bangladeshi media continued to face a high level of violence and harassment at the hands of the state and other actors in 2003. Although the constitution provides for freedom of expression subject to "reasonable restrictions," the press is constrained by national security legislation as well as sedition and criminal libel laws. In June, warrants of arrest were filed against two leading news editors for defamation after they published a letter that was critical of a senior government official. The Committee to Protect Journalists documented several other cases in which journalists who reported on crimes committed by officials were detained in reprisal on trumped-up charges. Journalists are regularly threatened and violently attacked by organized-crime groups, political parties and their supporters, government authorities, the police, and Islamist groups. Most commonly, they are subjected to such attacks as a result of their coverage of corruption, criminal activity, political violence, the rise of Islamic fundamentalism, or human rights abuses. Impunity for those who perpetrate crimes against journalists is the norm. The independent print media present diverse views, although coverage of politics at a number of newspapers is highly partisan. In addition, many journalists practice some level of self-censorship. The state owns most broadcast media, and coverage favors the ruling party. Political considerations influence the distribution of government advertising revenue and subsidized newsprint, upon which most publications are dependent. Authorities remained sensitive to scrutiny by the foreign media; in July they banned an issue of *Newsweek* that contained an article on the Koran, and foreign journalists have encountered increasing difficulties in obtaining visas to enter Bangladesh.

Barbados

Status: Free

Legal Environment: 4
Political Environment: 6
Economic Environment: 7
Total Score: 17

The press is free, diverse, and critical of government policies. Journalists operate in a relatively open environment; public opinion expressed in the media exerts significant influence on policy. There are four private and two state radio stations. Two independently owned daily newspapers present a variety of political opinions. Although the country's single television station is run by the government-owned Caribbean Broadcasting Corporation, it regularly reports views opposing state policies. Some reports, however, indicate that the government uses its influence to limit coverage of certain sensitive issues. Nongovernmental media ownership is somewhat concentrated, but no other significant economic influences restrict press freedom.

Belarus

Status: Not Free

Legal Environment: 26
Political Environment: 30
Economic Environment: 28
Total Score: 84

The condition of press freedom in Belarus remains dire. Although the constitution formally provides for freedom of speech, authorities are extremely intolerant of criticism, often silencing opposition media with libel lawsuits, financial pressures, closures and suspensions, and intimidation of journalists. An executive decree of President Alyaksandr Lukashenka prohibits activities that demean state authorities, and defamation of the president can result in up to five years in prison. The ministry of information controls the licensing of the print and broadcast media, regularly monitors media content, and often acts to stifle the independent press. A new Law on Mass Media presented to the parliament in October 2003 may serve to restrain press freedom in Belarus further, raising the specter of media re-registration and censorship of the Internet, among other restrictions. In May, the popular independent daily *Belorusskaya Delovaya Gazeta* was suspended for three months after receiving several warnings from the ministry of information concerning unfavorable coverage of the president and his government. All nationally available broadcast media are government owned, and authorities greatly restricted access to previously available Russian radio and television broadcasts in 2003. Journalists are subject to legal and physical harassment, and self-censorship is common. While, unlike the year before, no journalists were imprisoned in 2003, several were charged with libel and forced to pay large, often debilitating fines. In March, journalists Mikola Markevich and Pavel Mazheika were granted early releases after each had served six months of their respective corrective labor sentences following convictions for libel of the president in 2002.

Belgium

LEGAL ENVIRONMENT: 2
POLITICAL ENVIRONMENT: 3
ECONOMIC ENVIRONMENT: 4

Status: Free

TOTAL SCORE: 9

The media enjoy strong constitutional protections. Restrictions on libel, pornography, and the promotion of racial or religious discrimination have only a minor effect on press freedom. In July 2003, the European Court of Human Rights ruled in favor of protection of journalists' sources in a case involving police searches of media offices and journalists' homes in 1995. In January, the presenter of Radio Salam, an Arab-language radio station, was arrested for inciting violence against the non-Muslim population. Dual oversight boards seek to maintain balanced reporting on government-controlled radio and television networks. The press is highly concentrated among a few owners.

LEGAL ENVIRONMENT: 8
POLITICAL ENVIRONMENT: 9

Belize

ECONOMIC ENVIRONMENT: 5

Status: Free

TOTAL SCORE: 22

The constitution provides for freedom of press and speech, and the government generally respects these rights. However, the constitution also permits government authorities to make "reasonable provisions" in the interests of defense, public safety, public order, public morality, or public health. These provisions include fines and prison terms for any citizen who questions, outside strict procedural guidelines, any financial disclosure statements submitted by public officials. No cases limiting press freedom through these provisions were reported in 2003. Constraining libel laws cover both newspaper and television broadcasting, although these laws have not been applied in several years. Public debate, criticism, and comments on the government and political matters are vibrantly visible in the media. There are at least 10 privately owned weekly newspapers, two of which are owned by major political parties. Commercial radio stations are also plentiful, and state-run radio was privatized in 1998. Investigative journalist Melvin Flores fled to the United States in February 2003 after receiving threats, presumably related to his reports on a stolen U.S.-owned Hummer sport utility vehicle that was brought into Belize, allegedly with the help of government officials.

LEGAL ENVIRONMENT: 9
POLITICAL ENVIRONMENT: 11

Benin

ECONOMIC ENVIRONMENT: 10

Status: Free

TOTAL SCORE: 30

Constitutional guarantees of freedom of speech are largely respected in practice. However, a 1997 criminal libel law is occasionally used against journalists. Such was the case on April 1, 2003, when four journalists of *Le Telegramme* were detained and beaten by police who accused them of publishing a letter critical of police authorities. Benin's private press observed a "day without media" on April 7 to protest the incident. While the High Authority for Audio-Visual Media and Communications, a government entity, is responsible for oversight of media operations, media outlets are relatively free to criticize the government without interference.

Benin has an active and growing privately owned press with more than 20 daily newspapers, 30 private radio stations, and several broadcast television stations. A national new information and communication technologies policy was adopted in February 2003. Despite a prolific and independent press, journalistic integrity occasionally falls victim to bribery and blackmail as a result of financial pressures.

Bhutan

Status: Not Free

LEGAL ENVIRONMENT: 22
POLITICAL ENVIRONMENT: 24
ECONOMIC ENVIRONMENT: 22
TOTAL SCORE: 68

The government restricts freedom of expression, prohibiting criticism of King Wangchuk and of Bhutan's political system. The media in this small mountain kingdom are relatively underdeveloped; Bhutan has one regularly published newspaper, the weekly *Kuensel*, and broadcast media are under state control. Although it is now privately run, *Kuensel* generally reports news that puts the kingdom in a favorable light and avoids sensitive issues such as the refugee problem or corruption. An exception is occasional coverage of criticism by National Assembly members of government policies during assembly meetings. Similarly, state-run broadcast media do not carry opposition positions and statements. Cable television services, which carry uncensored foreign programming, are thriving. Internet access is growing and is largely unrestricted, although Druknet, the only ISP, does censor certain sites.

Bolivia

Status: Partly Free

LEGAL ENVIRONMENT: 13
POLITICAL ENVIRONMENT: 17
ECONOMIC ENVIRONMENT: 7
TOTAL SCORE: 37

Status change explanation: Bolivia's status has been lowered from Free to Partly Free due to the increase in repression, threats, and acts of violence against journalists from both the government and opposition forces during the course of the recent uprising.

The constitution provides for freedom of expression, but the government's commitment to this ideal was tested during the year. After the signing of the Declaration of Chapultepec in 2002, the political and social turmoil of 2003 caused backsliding in terms of press freedom. Most newspapers are privately owned, and many have an antigovernment stance. Low literacy levels mean that for many people the main source of news is the radio, and there are both state-owned and privately run stations. The polarization of the media became more evident as the social upheaval that resulted in the end of Gonzalo Sanchez de Losada's presidency unfolded. Both the opposition and the government attempted to influence public opinion through media reports. In addition to the existing strict slander and defamation laws, the chaotic political situation in Bolivia led to an increasingly difficult environment for journalists. The number of journalists attacked and threatened by both government agents and civilian protesters increased significantly. Two radio stations were bombed, and there were attempts to censor newspapers' coverage of the popular uprising. Privately owned antigovernment media outlets were accused of inciting violence and acts of treason but were not prosecuted. Journalists at a state-owned television station resigned in protest after being pressured not to show images of violence. A 40-member independent press tribunal is currently responsible for evaluating whether or not journalists' practices violate the constitution or citizens' rights. Due to government proposals to establish a regulatory agency for the media as well as pressure from the courts, journalists at times practice self-censorship.

Bosnia-Herzegovina

Status: Partly Free

LEGAL ENVIRONMENT: 9
POLITICAL ENVIRONMENT: 20
ECONOMIC ENVIRONMENT: 19
TOTAL SCORE: 48

Freedom of expression is a key feature of both the constitution and the Human Rights Annex to the Dayton Peace Accords. However, the media landscape of Bosnia and Herzegovina remains complex: Ruling political structures put pressure on the media; the ethnic division of the country poses an obstacle to the free flow of information; local and foreign investment in the media is insufficient; and press laws and media regulations are still being developed. Although defamation and slander were decriminalized in 2003, many individuals and institutions file civil defamation suits against media outlets asking for excessive compensation. Print media are characterized by strong divisions along ethnic and ideological lines. Currently 7 dailies are published, and more than 30 TV stations, of which 12 are public, are broadcasting. Most of the 97 private and 46 public radio stations are local, despite the existence of some nationwide stations. While some local radio stations carry independent news programming, most either limit their broadcasts to entertainment or focus on local political and ethnic interests. Although some cases of verbal harassment of journalists occurred in 2003, physical attacks on journalists were less frequent than in previous years. There is no official censorship body, but a regional court indirectly censored the media by imposing a temporary measure forbidding the top-rated daily *Dnevni Avaz* to write about Hilmo Selimovic, the director and major shareholder of the Sarajevo Brewery. A similar measure prevented the daily *Dani* from writing about Fahrudin Radoncic, owner of *Avaz*. Authorities continue to direct advertising revenue from government-owned companies away from critical news outlets.

Botswana

Status: Free

LEGAL ENVIRONMENT: 6
POLITICAL ENVIRONMENT: 14
ECONOMIC ENVIRONMENT: 10
TOTAL SCORE: 30

Freedom of speech and of the press is enshrined in the constitution, and the government generally respects these rights in practice. A small but robust independent press is often critical of the government but has recently encountered censorship and libel suits. The state dominates broadcast media, despite recent inroads by private enterprise. Government critics and the political opposition allege that they have insufficient access to these outlets, which explicitly support government policies and actions. In November, the government suspended a segment of Radio Botswana's popular morning show *Masa-a-sele*, previously used by opposition parties to attack the government. In retaliation for their critical reporting, several journalists were threatened or attacked.

LEGAL ENVIRONMENT: 10
POLITICAL ENVIRONMENT: 16

Brazil

ECONOMIC ENVIRONMENT: 10

Status: Partly Free

TOTAL SCORE: 36

The country, South America's largest media market, enjoys a vibrant and active press. The constitution guarantees a free press, and the media provide vigorous reporting on controversial issues and government performance. There are hundreds of newspapers and television channels and more than a thousand radio stations. However, media ownership is highly concentrated, with such companies as Globo dominating the market in both print and broadcast media. The government has licensing authority, and some politicians frequently obtain licenses; former congressional members overseeing communications are reported to own many broadcast and print media outlets. According to the Committee to Protect Journalists, during the year the government telecommunications agency, ANATEL, closed many community radio stations that were operating without a license; however, more than 4,000 small radio stations complained that they had applied for licenses in 2003 without any response from the agency. The ministry of communications responded by creating a working group to investigate these complaints. There has been an increase in defamation lawsuits and an increasing trend of plaintiffs seeking high reparation awards. The National Newspaper Association, citing the huge fines for libel and possible jail sentences, has pushed for an updated press law. High on the radar screen among journalists in Brazil is the increasing incidence of violence and harassment against journalists. Four journalists were killed over a period of two months in 2003, and two journalists were killed in 2002. Many international press advocacy organizations claim that Brazil, especially in the rural areas, is one of the most dangerous Latin American countries for the practice of journalism in terms of attacks, threats, pressures, and obstruction of information.

Brunei

Status: Not Free

LEGAL ENVIRONMENT: 27
POLITICAL ENVIRONMENT: 25
ECONOMIC ENVIRONMENT: 22
TOTAL SCORE: 74

Freedoms of speech and of the press are significantly restricted under emergency laws that have been in effect since 1962. Legislation introduced in 2001 allows officials to shut down newspapers without showing cause and to fine and jail journalists who write or publish articles deemed "false and malicious." In addition, newspapers must apply for annual publishing permits, and noncitizens are required to obtain government approval before working for media outlets. The English-language daily *News Express* closed in 2002 after being sued successfully by a private law firm for defamation. The only local broadcast media are operated by the government-controlled Radio Television Brunei, whose coverage favors the regime, although foreign programs are available on cable or satellite channels. The largest daily, the *Borneo Bulletin*, practices self-censorship, though it does publish letters to the editor that criticize government policies. Internet use is growing and provides another avenue for citizens to express critical opinions. However, the Internet forum BruneiTalk was temporarily blocked in May 2003 after contributors discussed the business dealings of senior officials.

Bulgaria

Status: Partly Free

LEGAL ENVIRONMENT: 10
POLITICAL ENVIRONMENT: 13
ECONOMIC ENVIRONMENT: 12
TOTAL SCORE: 35

Status change explanation: Bulgaria's status declined from Free to Partly Free to reflect increased government influence over public media outlets as well as a rise in the use of libel suits against journalists and publishers.

The most serious problems in the Bulgarian media landscape are political control over state broadcasters, a politicized process of allocating licenses, and manipulation of advertising, which threatens the position of independent media, especially at the local and regional levels. Coercion of the press comes both from the government and from criminal organizations. In November, the government proposed amendments to the criminal code that would have made it a crime for anyone, including journalists, to disclose classified information, even if it served the public interest or caused no harm to national security interests, an approach that is inconsistent with European standards. After protests by local and international NGOs, parliament dropped the proposals. Libel and defamation are considered criminal offenses, and although prison sentences as a penalty for libel have been eliminated, journalists charged with libel are penalized with high fines. Local watchdog groups have expressed concern that the number of suits brought against journalists by the government has been increasing in recent years. Violence against journalists still exists, mostly due to organized crime and the climate of impunity fostered by a weak judiciary. A number of journalists were attacked in 2003 as a result of their investigation into the underworld. In such an environment, many journalists practice self-censorship; investigative journalism about corruption and organized crime is rare. There are nine nationwide dailies (two of which are controlled by the German concern Westdeutsche Allgemeine Zeitung (WAZ)), two nationwide weeklies, and more than 50 local dailies and weeklies. WAZ monopolizes the newspaper market through dumping policies on prices, distribution, and advertising. There are three national television stations, two private ones, and the public broadcaster, Bulgarian National Television, which is perceived to be under the control of the ruling coalition and to lack editorial independence.

Burkina Faso

Status: Partly Free

LEGAL ENVIRONMENT: 11
POLITICAL ENVIRONMENT: 15
ECONOMIC ENVIRONMENT: 13
TOTAL SCORE: 39

Freedom of speech is protected by the constitution, and the government generally respects this right in practice. Under the 1993 information code, media outlets accused of endangering national security or distributing false news can be summarily banned. The Supreme Council of Information, a state-run media supervisory body, regulates the broadcast media. State-operated media outlets display a considerable degree of pro-government bias. In contrast, the independent media, including several daily newspapers and more than 50 radio stations, function with little governmental interference, are able to report on issues such as corruption or human rights violations, and are often critical of the government. However, the administration remains sensitive to scrutiny and pressures some journalists into practicing self-censorship. Reporters are occasionally subjected to harassment at the hands of police. In February, police in Bobo-Dioulasso briefly detained the editor of the independent daily *L'Express Du Faso* after he refused to reveal his source for a story concerning the local police. Access to foreign media broadcasts and to the Internet is unrestricted.

Burma (Myanmar)

Status: Not Free

LEGAL ENVIRONMENT: 30
POLITICAL ENVIRONMENT: 38
ECONOMIC ENVIRONMENT: 27
TOTAL SCORE: 95

The ruling military junta continues to restrict press freedom tightly. A 1996 decree banning speech or statements that "undermine national stability" remains in effect and is zealously implemented. Other laws require private publications to apply for annual licenses and criminalize the use of unregistered telecommunications equipment, computers, and software. In November, Zaw Thet Htway, an editor of *First Eleven*, was arrested and convicted of treason after the sports magazine published articles dealing with corruption in local sports. A number of other journalists and writers remained in jail throughout the year as a result of expressing dissident views. The small number of foreign reporters, allowed to enter Burma only on special visas, are subjected to intense scrutiny while in the country. Although there are harsh penalties for anyone caught listening to them, foreign radio broadcasts remain a primary source of balanced news for many Burmese, according to the Committee to Protect Journalists. The government owns all broadcast media and daily newspapers and exercises tight control over a growing number of weekly and monthly publications. It subjects private periodicals to prepublication censorship and limits coverage to a small range of permissible topics. While official media outlets serve as mouthpieces of the state, private media generally avoid political news, and many journalists practice self-censorship. Local media were forbidden to report on a banking crisis in February 2003, and coverage of the May 30 crackdown on Aung San Suu Kyi and her National League for Democracy party was limited to pro-government propaganda. A stagnant economy and limited market for advertising revenue (following a 2002 ban on advertising Thai products) threatens the financial viability of the private press. The BBC reported that publishers faced additional difficulties when the price of newsprint rose by almost 50 percent following the imposition of U.S. sanctions in July.

Burundi
Status: Not Free

LEGAL ENVIRONMENT: 21
POLITICAL ENVIRONMENT: 30
ECONOMIC ENVIRONMENT: 24
TOTAL SCORE: 75

Although the transitional constitution provides for freedom of expression, the government restricts this right in practice. While a new press law, enacted in late 2003, has been hailed by journalists as an improvement, it continues to authorize prepublication censorship and greatly restricts the media's ability to report on sensitive issues and express views that diverge from those of the government. The state-run National Communication Council, which is charged with regulating the media, occasionally bans or suspends independent publications and restricts permissible reporting. In March 2003, all radio stations were barred from broadcasting interviews with or messages from two rebel groups. As a result, the government temporarily suspended Radio Insanganiro in September for airing an interview with a rebel group spokesman, accusing the station of "endangering national unity." The suspension sparked protest from other independent media. Nevertheless, three days later the government suspended Radio Publique Africaine (RPA) for a similar offense. In addition, reporters remain vulnerable to official harassment, detention, and violence, and many practice self-censorship. The government owns and operates the main broadcast media as well as the country's only regularly published newspaper. Private publications and radio stations function sporadically, but some, such as RPA, manage to present diverse and balanced views.

Cambodia
Status: Not Free

LEGAL ENVIRONMENT: 19
POLITICAL ENVIRONMENT: 22
ECONOMIC ENVIRONMENT: 22
TOTAL SCORE: 63

Freedoms of expression, the press, and publication are provided for in the constitution, and the government publicly professes to support these rights. However, although the press law provides journalists with several safeguards, it also permits the information ministry to suspend newspapers, broadly prohibits the publication of articles that affect national security and political stability, and subjects the press to criminal statutes. In recent years, authorities have used the press law to suspend several newspapers for 30-day periods for criticizing the government or monarchy. Moreover, the government in January detained a newspaper editor, and the owner of Cambodia's sole independent radio station, on charges of inciting anti-Thai riots by allegedly publishing or broadcasting unchecked rumors. Officials who made inflammatory statements during the incident did not face prosecution. Print journalists, who are freer than their broadcast counterparts, routinely criticize government policies and senior officials. Most broadcast media are controlled by the state, according to the World Press Freedom Committee, and programming favors the ruling party. Prior to the July elections, local watchdog groups noted that people were warned not to listen to foreign radio broadcasts and that opposition parties were not given adequate access to broadcast media outlets. Authorities have also denied repeated requests from opposition leader Sam Rainsy for a radio station license. The majority of private media outlets receive funding or subsidies from members of political parties. Journalists face some threats and harassment by the state and other actors. In October, unknown assailants killed Chuor Chetharith, an editor with an opposition radio station in Phnom Penh.

Cameroon

LEGAL ENVIRONMENT: 21
POLITICAL ENVIRONMENT: 25
ECONOMIC ENVIRONMENT: 21

Status: Not Free

TOTAL SCORE: 67

Although the constitution includes safeguards for freedom of expression and of the press, these rights are severely restricted in practice by an assortment of punitive laws. The penal code prescribes lengthy prison terms and hefty fines for contempt, defamation, or dissemination of false news after a fair trial in a court of law. In reality, however, overzealous police officers harass and detain critical journalists at will, or even shut down news outlets deemed too critical of the ruling elite. While the authorities insist that press freedom is real in Cameroon, media speculation about the planned October 2004 presidential election has proved a risky undertaking, and journalists admitted to practicing increasing levels of self-censorship in the run-up to the elections. Most of the government's censorship was aimed at the fledgling private broadcasting sector; the authorities regularly resorted to overwhelming police force to shutter private broadcast operations, many of which are not fully licensed or exist at the pleasure of the state. Little legal progress has been achieved since 2001, when President Paul Biya signed into law a decade-old bill liberalizing the electronic media, and the state-owned Cameroon Radio and Television remains the only fully licensed broadcaster. With the approaching election, greater agitation in the opposition, and increased press speculation about Biya's ability to remain in office after 21 years, the government has taken to invoking harsh libel laws and stringent licensing requirements to shut down critical electronic media outlets. At year's end, the authorities had still not released even partial broadcasting licenses to dozens of applicants, most of whom have been waiting since 2001. Meanwhile, the government's touchiness about press coverage of long-lasting tensions between the French-speaking majority and the Anglophone southwestern minorities continues to inhibit the media's ability to address tribalism and regionalism, two increasingly prominent features of local politics.

Canada

LEGAL ENVIRONMENT: 2
POLITICAL ENVIRONMENT: 7
ECONOMIC ENVIRONMENT: 6

Status: Free

TOTAL SCORE: 15

Under Canada's Constitution Act of 1982, the Charter of Rights and Freedoms provides constitutional protection for freedom of expression, including freedom of the press. Defamatory libel and blasphemous libel are criminal offenses according to the federal criminal code. There are no laws regulating the distribution of print media. Press freedom in Canada has declined slightly in recent years due to increasing concentration of media ownership. Media in Canada are generally free, though they sometimes exercise self-censorship in areas such as violence on television. Some civil libertarians have expressed concern over an amendment to the criminal code giving judges wide latitude in determining what constitutes hate speech on the Internet. In February 2003, press freedom groups criticized Bill C-20, an act to amend Canada's criminal code to combat child pornography. The groups said the amendment provided greater powers for law enforcement to seize materials from private citizens and that it threatened artistic expression. In June, press freedom groups criticized a Quebec City court for signing search warrants that would allow police to seize video recordings from several television stations as part of an investigation into a teenage prostitution case. In December, Canadian Journalists for Free Expression called on Ontario's attorney general to cease criminal proceedings against author Stephen Williams. Williams wrote two books critical of police investigations into serial killings of young women in the 1990s, in alleged violation of a publication ban. Police had earlier raided Williams's home, confiscating computer equipment.

Cape Verde

Status: Partly Free

LEGAL ENVIRONMENT: 8
POLITICAL ENVIRONMENT: 16
ECONOMIC ENVIRONMENT: 12
TOTAL SCORE: 36

Status change explanation: Cape Verde's rating fell from Free to Partly Free to reflect the continued influence of the government over the broadcast media and of the ruling party over the privately owned media, both of which have contributed to reports of growing self-censorship among journalists.

Press freedom is guaranteed in the constitution and is generally respected by the government. A 1999 constitutional amendment excludes the use of freedom of expression as a defense in defamation cases. In November 2002, the newspaper *A Semana* was charged with and found guilty of defamation for an article that accused judges and public prosecutors of accepting bribes. At the end of 2003, this case was still under appeal with the Supreme Court. While the law requires a formal licensing mechanism for mass media, no government authorization is needed for print publications. There are three independent newspapers and one state-owned newspaper. Cape Verde also has one government-owned and six independent radio stations and one state- and two foreign-owned television stations. However, the ruling African Party for the Independence of Cape Verde continues to control the main privately owned news media while the government dominates television broadcasting. The past year has seen reports of growing self-censorship on the part of journalists working at privately owned media outlets. This trend may be accentuated by the fact that in a stagnant economic environment, many journalists are able to find only short-term contract employment at state-owned media agencies that do not criticize the government.

LEGAL ENVIRONMENT: 25
POLITICAL ENVIRONMENT: 22
Central African Republic
ECONOMIC ENVIRONMENT: 17

Status: Not Free   TOTAL SCORE: 64

Until it was suspended in the wake of the March coup d'etat that brought Army commander Francois Bozize to power, the constitution guaranteed freedom of expression, even though this right had often been brutally restricted by previous regimes. Citing the country's harsh press laws, the deposed government of President Ange-Felix Patasse frequently targeted outspoken journalists for forced exile, arbitrary detentions, and legal and physical harassment. In a country plagued by chronic instability, the press was nearly unanimous in its support for the coup d'etat by Bozize, who released from unlawful detention opposition figures, journalists, and free speech advocates jailed by the Patasse government. The new regime has planned a constitutional referendum and general elections for late 2004, to which the private press has been assured unfettered access, a privilege routinely denied it by the ousted regime. In addition, official press conferences are now open to all journalists. In the fall, the new Bozize government slated a "National Dialogue" whose final recommendations included a revision of the press laws, the establishment of an independent media regulatory body, and the creation of a university-level journalism curriculum. Even so, there were instances of police harassment of news professionals. The judiciary, still relying on punitive press laws enacted under Patasse, sentenced at least one journalist to prison for his work. In November, a group of private journalists and editors began a push to convince the authorities of the necessity to decriminalize press offenses. Nevertheless, hope was slim that the press laws would be improved or scrapped in the near future, and self-censorship among journalists appeared to be on the rise.

Chad

Status: Not Free

LEGAL ENVIRONMENT: 24
POLITICAL ENVIRONMENT: 29
ECONOMIC ENVIRONMENT: 21
TOTAL SCORE: 74

Freedom of expression and of the press is protected under the constitution, but government practices routinely place journalists at risk of suspension, detention, and legal and physical harassment for their work. Newspapers critical of the government circulate freely in the capital, N'Djamena, but their impact is very limited in the rest of the country where radio remains the most efficient medium of public information. The government's mistrust of prospective broadcasters seriously impairs the growth of private electronic media. But despite constant official scrutiny and high licensing fees for commercial radio, some stations continue to operate, and the number of stations run by nonprofit groups has reportedly increased. The High Council on Communication (HCC), despite having sole legal authority to enforce broadcasting rules, is often ignored by government ministries and officials who prefer to take direct actions against offending broadcasters. Harsh libel laws remain on the books and are widely invoked to inhibit press criticism of the elite; at least two journalists from the private weekly *Notre Temps* were charged with criminal libel during the year. The authorities also filed a complaint with the HCC against Radio FM Liberte for reporting on fast-spreading insecurity, only to shut down the station before the HCC could deliberate. While journalists' access to government-held information is severely restricted, there were fewer reports of arbitrary reprisals for publishing material on an active rebellion in the northern Tibesti region during the year. Meanwhile, Radio Brakos, which was closed down in 2002, was allowed to resume broadcasting. Television remains the exclusive domain of the state, largely because of the high cost and the likelihood of modest returns on operating a private television channel in this impoverished desert nation.

Chile

Status: Free

LEGAL ENVIRONMENT: 8
POLITICAL ENVIRONMENT: 7
ECONOMIC ENVIRONMENT: 8
TOTAL SCORE: 23

The Chilean constitution provides for freedom of speech; media are independent and continue to cover sensitive issues and criticize the government. Journalists generally operate free from physical threats and intimidation, but the continued presence of insult laws still poses a problem for those reporting on government and military figures. Defamation suits are common and in one case led to the censorship of a television program. Nevertheless, media report extensively on the human rights abuses that occurred under the 17-year Pinochet regime and have uncovered large corruption scandals in which the present government and the private sector were implicated. Most print media outlets, although independent of the government, are owned by one of two major media groups. State-owned print and broadcast media are usually able to remain editorially independent. However, in May 2003, editorial staff at *La Nacion Domingo,* maintaining that the management had bowed to political pressure, resigned in protest at the paper's decision to delay publication of an investigative story on alleged official corruption.

China

Status: Not Free

LEGAL ENVIRONMENT: 27
POLITICAL ENVIRONMENT: 32
ECONOMIC ENVIRONMENT: 21
TOTAL SCORE: 80

China's authoritarian regime continues to place widespread restrictions on freedoms of the press and of expression. A combination of formal statutes and informal directives forbids media outlets from promoting political reform, covering internal party politics or the inner workings of government, criticizing Beijing's domestic and international policies, or reporting financial data that the government has not released. However, after a recent transfer of power to a younger generation of leaders, officials more frequently allow journalists to report on local corruption and other ills that the party itself seeks to alleviate. Because all stories are potentially subject to prepublication censorship, many reporters avoid certain topics or otherwise practice self-censorship. At the end of the year, Chinese jails held 39 journalists, including one South Korean, according to the Committee to Protect Journalists. Other journalists have been harassed, detained, threatened, or dismissed from their jobs because of their reporting. Officials also have suspended or shut down some magazines, newspapers, and publishing houses. While China's print media are both public and private, the state owns and operates all radio and television stations; coverage on the broadcast media promotes the government line.

Nevertheless, talk radio and lively tabloid newspapers flourish in many Chinese cities. Hoping to encourage greater financial self-sufficiency, the government introduced regulations requiring all publications to earn at least half of their revenue from subscriptions, and shortly thereafter authorities closed 673 unprofitable state-funded newspapers and periodicals. The government promotes use of the Internet, which it believes to be critical to China's economic development, but regulates access, monitors use, and restricts and regulates content. Journalists, students, and political dissidents are at times detained or jailed for Internet-related offenses. Hong Kong's traditionally free press continues to be relatively outspoken, although many media outlets practice some self-censorship when reporting on Chinese politics, powerful local business interests, and calls for Taiwanese or Tibetan independence. During the year, a broad range of civil society groups, business interests, and citizens managed to block implementation of the controversial Article 23 national security legislation through sustained campaigning and street protests.

Colombia

Status: Not Free

LEGAL ENVIRONMENT: 12
POLITICAL ENVIRONMENT: 32
ECONOMIC ENVIRONMENT: 19
TOTAL SCORE: 63

Colombia's ongoing, 40-year-old civil war has not abated. The precarious security situation prevailing throughout the country extends especially to journalists covering the conflict between the government's military forces, heavily armed drug-trafficking groups, and various paramilitary rebel organizations, particularly FARC, a leftist guerrilla group that retains effective political control of many areas in southern Colombia. Established laws are relatively supportive of a free press, and the media is actively critical of the government and civil rebel groups, but the national government, led by President Alvaro Uribe, lacks the political control to enforce these laws effectively. Consequently, violent reprisals and abductions are commonly perpetrated against reporters documenting human rights abuses in the civil war or the activities of drug traffickers in the region. In 2003, 4 journalists were murdered and 40 more received death threats, making Colombia one of the most dangerous countries in the world for journalists. A considerable amount of self-censorship results from this insecure environment. Reporting in FARC-controlled areas is close to nonexistent. After two reporters for the *Los Angeles Times* were kidnapped in January, the reach of the insecurity problem is understood to extend even to foreign journalists covering the conflict. Media companies in Colombia have consolidated into huge conglomerates, all of which are owned by business groups with close ties to the political establishment. The consolidations have served to limit the range of opinion available to news consumers: these mega-companies control 80 percent of television and radio broadcasters, as well as the only newspaper with a national circulation, *El Tiempo*.

Comoros

LEGAL ENVIRONMENT: 12
POLITICAL ENVIRONMENT: 20
ECONOMIC ENVIRONMENT: 13

Status: Partly Free

TOTAL SCORE: 45

A new constitution adopted in December 2001 provides for freedom of speech and of the press, and these rights are generally respected. Nevertheless, journalists are occasionally sued for defamation. The semiofficial weekly *Al-Watwan* and several private newspapers are published regularly. Although the independent print and broadcast media operate without overt government interference and are critical of official policies, some journalists are believed to exercise self-censorship. Reporters are occasionally harassed; in September a French journalist was arrested and charged with attempting a coup. Lack of resources is a major impediment to a more robust media in Comoros.

Congo, Republic of (Brazzaville)

LEGAL ENVIRONMENT: 17
POLITICAL ENVIRONMENT: 20
ECONOMIC ENVIRONMENT: 17

Status: Partly Free

TOTAL SCORE: 54

No press freedom abuses were recorded in 2003 in the Republic of Congo, where the constitution provides for freedom of the press but criminalizes certain types of journalistic speech such as incitement to ethnic hatred, violence, or civil war. Since the official end of the civil war in March 2002, the government has generally respected the rights of journalists to seek and impart information but continues to monopolize broadcast media.

Cases of official abuse of journalists' rights to report the news have been on the decline since 2000, when the government officially abolished censorship and sharply reduced penalties for defamation. The improved press law, which also applies to the Internet and business public relations operations, imposes monetary penalties for defamation and incitement to violence but no longer requires prison terms for violators. The peace agreement and an ongoing national reconciliation drive appear to have fostered a new spirit of objectivity among a press corps splintered along ethnic lines during the civil war. While the state is not known to own or to control print publications directly, half a dozen private newspapers appearing weekly in the capital, Brazzaville, carry strongly pro-government editorials. Another half-dozen criticize the authorities freely and often print acerbic position papers from jailed or exiled opposition figures. However, print media do not circulate widely beyond Brazzaville and other densely populated areas, leaving most Congolese to rely on radio broadcasts for information on local and international events.

Congo, Democratic Republic of (Kinshasa)

Status: Not Free

LEGAL ENVIRONMENT: 25
POLITICAL ENVIRONMENT: 31
ECONOMIC ENVIRONMENT: 24

TOTAL SCORE: 80

Repeated rephrasing of the constitution has left untouched the clauses on freedom of expression and of the press, but in practice Congolese journalists lack legal protections in the exercise of their profession, and their rights are consistently suppressed. In its current, transitional version, the constitution mandates that a high authority on media be created to serve as guarantor of the right to freedom of expression and a watchdog of journalistic ethics. But the authority, which parliament must approve, has not yet been created, more than a year after a power-sharing deal between government and rebel forces officially ended the conflict. The current press law, enacted under the late dictator Mobutu Sesse Seko, criminalizes criticism of state officials and requires publishers to deposit copies of their publications with the ministry of communication and press on the day of publication. Common press offenses include defamation, false news, "endangering the State," and "insulting the military" through publication or broadcast of political news or news about the war. Under Laurent-Desire Kabila, who ruled from May 1997 until January 2001, the Court of Military Order prosecuted such violations, some of which could result in the death penalty. Aggressive coverage of war issues or of government corruption still draws serious consequences. Members of the media are routinely arrested, detained, beaten, harassed, and intimidated, and copies of their newspapers are seized by civil or armed loyalists of President Joseph Kabila's People's Party for Reconstruction and Development (PPRD). Journalists do not fare any better in the regions under rebel control or at the hands of the various foreign armies backing the local warring parties. Throughout this vast war-ravaged country, physical attacks on the press are often the work of powerful public figures— businesspeople, and government, military, and rebel officials—who reportedly enlist soldiers and police officers with bribes. For want of a functioning state structure, journalists cannot always seek redress, and perpetrators, even when identified, go unpunished. When arrested for alleged press offenses, few journalists are formally charged or tried in court. Some have been jailed without charge for more than three months. Due to limited literacy, radio is the most important medium. There are 24 private or religious radio stations; the government runs 2. It also runs 2 television stations; private companies, civil opposition, and rebel and religious groups control another 20. Although less virulent in their criticism of the government, the electronic media are no less subject to official abuse. Charges of faulty licenses, shady finances, and unpaid taxes or imposition of unfairly high taxes have been used to intimidate private stations.

Costa Rica

LEGAL ENVIRONMENT: 7
POLITICAL ENVIRONMENT: 7
ECONOMIC ENVIRONMENT: 5

Status: Free

TOTAL SCORE: 19

Costa Rica's independent media scene is vibrant, with numerous private newspapers and television stations and more than 50 radio stations. However, a survey conducted by *La Nacion* newspaper of 184 journalists and their perception of press freedom revealed significant constraints journalists feel they face in reporting freely. The survey indicated that 41 percent said they purposely left out information in reporting due to legal concerns and 79 percent said they felt pressure not to investigate certain issues. Libel, slander, and defamation are criminal rather than civil offenses, and people have a "right to reply" and sue media if they feel their reputation has been impugned by a matter of news. Two gunmen killed journalist Ivannia Mora Rodriguez in December 2003; allegations of the assassination centered on her former boss, the owner of the magazine *Estrategia y Negocios*. Her killing was the second press-related killing in two years and raised alarm among press freedom advocates. In a victory for press freedom, the Inter-American Court of Human Rights ruled that it would hear the case of journalist Mauricio Herrera Ulloa, who was convicted of criminal defamation in 1999; if his conviction is overturned, Costa Rica, as a member state of the Court, would be ordered to bring its criminal defamation laws closer in line with international standards.

Cote d'Ivoire

LEGAL ENVIRONMENT: 19
POLITICAL ENVIRONMENT: 29
ECONOMIC ENVIRONMENT: 17

Status: Not Free

TOTAL SCORE: 65

As political instability continued to divide the country in 2003, access to balanced information was limited and Ivoirian as well as foreign media remained subject to threats and pressure both from the government and from rebel forces. Constitutional provisions for freedom of expression are not always respected in practice. The law allows authorities to initiate criminal libel proceedings against persons who insult the president or prime minister, defame institutions of the state, or undermine the reputation of the nation. However, the government has announced its intention to introduce draft legislation that would eliminate prison sentences for press offenses. Dozens of independent newspapers, many of which have links to political parties, continue to criticize official policies freely, while state-owned newspapers and a state-run broadcasting system are usually unreservedly pro-government. Several private radio stations and a cable television service operate, but only the state broadcasting system reaches a national audience. There is liberal access to the Internet, and in February the government allowed Radio France Internationale (RFI), the BBC, and Africa No. 1 to resume their FM broadcasts after having suspended them five months previously. In such a partisan environment, journalists have been subjected to threats and attacks from all sides. A reporter for the state-run press agency was found murdered in western Cote d'Ivoire in March, and a correspondent for RFI was shot and killed by a policeman in October. Some monitoring groups expressed concern that an anti-French campaign in the pro-government media had been a contributing factor to the murder. In the same month, opposition newspapers temporarily halted publishing after pro-government militants attacked newspaper delivery trucks.

Croatia

Status: Partly Free

LEGAL ENVIRONMENT: 11
POLITICAL ENVIRONMENT: 12
ECONOMIC ENVIRONMENT: 14
TOTAL SCORE: 37

Press freedom is provided for in the constitution, but print media outlets tend to enjoy more editorial freedom than broadcast media; most television stations are still partially owned by the government and are strongly influenced by political pressures. The government still retains its nationwide monopoly on the main broadcast station, which was used heavily in the last decade as a vehicle for issuing nationalist propaganda by the Tudjman regime. Although there is a network of private media outlets, their ownership structure is largely non-transparent. The two national newspaper dailies are still majority-owned by the state and have not been privatized. Positively, a number of media laws were passed in 2003: the Law on Media; the Law on Electronic Media; the Law on Croatian Radio and Television (HRT); and the Law on the Right to Access Information. There was some criticism that the Law on Croatian Radio and Television, while representing an improvement over previous legislation, gave parliament too much control over the appointment of members to the HRT Broadcasting Council, which is responsible for regulating the media and awarding tenders. Additional criticism pointed to proposed amendments to the criminal code and press law that would have made it easier to prosecute journalists who criticized public figures. Journalists remain exposed to threats and violence; in March, a bomb was planted under the car of Nino Pavic, the co-owner of Europapress Holding (EPH), Croatia's largest independent newspaper publisher. In addition, a number of journalists at EPH's popular weekly, *Globus,* were threatened after the paper published a series of articles about the criminal activities of several mafia groups in the months preceding the bombing. Some journalists report self-censorship and that their access to information is denied, especially at the local level.

Cuba

LEGAL ENVIRONMENT: 30
POLITICAL ENVIRONMENT: 38
ECONOMIC ENVIRONMENT: 28

Status: Not Free

TOTAL SCORE: 96

After 45 years in power, Fidel Castro's government shows no sign of allowing independent voices to emerge in the Cuban media. On March 18, 2003, authorities arrested 27 independent journalists, all of whom were subsequently given sham trials and prison sentences of up to 28 years on charges of collaborating with "imperialist interests." Reporters Without Borders has since labeled Cuba "the world's largest prison for journalists." The spring crackdown took place in conjunction with the arrest of 50 dissident political activists, most of them prominent spokespeople for a citizens' initiative for democratic reform, the Varela Project. Consequently, the government has undone the small hints of progress toward press freedom in Cuba that had taken hold in 2002, when Jimmy Carter arrived on a state visit and gave an unprecedented live, nationally broadcast, televised speech offering praise of the dissident movement and independent press. Governments and human rights advocacy groups worldwide, including many prominent European leaders, joined in strongly condemning the arrests of these journalists and democratic activists by Castro's government. All media outlets in Cuba must be funded by the government, and all reporting is controlled for ideological content, which must be in agreement with official government positions. A few isolated independent journalists remain, but their situation is precarious, and they must practice self-censorship to avoid imprisonment.

Cyprus

LEGAL ENVIRONMENT: 4
POLITICAL ENVIRONMENT: 6
ECONOMIC ENVIRONMENT: 8

Status: Free

TOTAL SCORE: 18

Freedom of the press is generally respected in law and practice in the Greek sector. A vibrant independent press frequently criticizes authorities, and private television and radio stations compete effectively with government-controlled stations. Concentration of ownership is a problem, however, and proper laws have not been implemented to prevent it from increasing. Most daily newspapers belong to or are linked to political parties or other groups, and only the state broadcaster has sufficient funds for producing much of its own programming. Travel across the border between the north and the south was severely restricted in the past, but in April 2003 the Turkish Cypriot authorities ended the requirement that journalists purchase a visa for entry; still, journalists are required to wear an identification tag for certain events, and this year Greek Cypriot journalists chose not to cover these events. In the disputed north, laws are in place for freedom of the press, but authorities are overtly hostile to the independent press. Court cases were brought against many journalists this year, often for insulting the Turkish military, which has a large presence here. Many local daily newspapers are available, but the broadcasting service is exclusively controlled by the Turkish-Cypriot administration. [The numerical rating for Cyprus is based on conditions in the Greek side of the island.]

Czech Republic

LEGAL ENVIRONMENT: 6
POLITICAL ENVIRONMENT: 10
ECONOMIC ENVIRONMENT: 7

Status: Free

TOTAL SCORE: 23

Czech media are independent, and the government generally respects press freedom. However, the Charter of Fundamental Rights and Freedoms prohibits threats against individual rights, state and public security, public health, and morality, and libel can be prosecuted as a criminal offense. Primarily because of weak regulatory institutions and heavy influence on the media by political parties and business interests, the media are often seen as being politically aligned. The three-year ownership dispute between the government and American-owned Central European Media Enterprise (CME) ended in May, when an international arbitration court ruled that the government pay $359 million in damages to CME for failure to protect the company's controlling investment in the popular television station Nova. Foreign ownership in the press market also continues to be high: German and Swiss companies hold more than 80 percent of daily press outlets. Some press advocates assert that such foreign concentration diminishes the role the media plays as a public watchdog; foreign owners may not want to support investigative journalism vigorously, instead pushing for tabloid journalism that can bring in higher profits. The former secretary-general of the foreign ministry, Karel Srba, was convicted in June for plotting to murder Sabina Slonkova, a popular investigative journalist for the independent daily

Mlada Fronta Dnes. Srba had been forced to resign from his post in March 2001 after Slonkova reported stories on the foreign minister's suspicious operation of a hotel in Moscow.

Denmark
Status: Free

LEGAL ENVIRONMENT: 1	
POLITICAL ENVIRONMENT: 1	
ECONOMIC ENVIRONMENT: 6	
TOTAL SCORE: 8	

The media enjoy strong constitutional protections for free expression and a long tradition of press freedom. Independent print and broadcast media represent a wide variety of views and are frequently critical of the government. Although in 2002 Copenhagen police secretly recorded telephone conversations between journalist Stig Matthiesen and his editor at the newspaper *Jyllands-Posten,* a court order requiring Matthiesen to reveal his sources was subsequently overturned, as Danish law protects journalists from revealing confidential sources except in cases of serious crime or where necessary for police investigation. Tight restrictions on advertising for Danish broadcasters have led some broadcasters to move to Britain.

Djibouti
Status: Not Free

LEGAL ENVIRONMENT: 21	
POLITICAL ENVIRONMENT: 25	
ECONOMIC ENVIRONMENT: 20	
TOTAL SCORE: 66	

Despite constitutional protection, the government often restricts freedom of speech. Slander is prohibited, and other laws that prohibit the dissemination of "false information" and regulate the publication of newspapers have been used against the independent press. Although private publications are generally allowed to circulate freely and provide some criticism of official policies, journalists generally self-censor coverage of sensitive issues due to fear of prosecution. In 2003 opposition leader Daher Ahmed Farah, the director of the independent newspaper *Le Renouveau,* was arrested, detained, and released from custody on four separate occasions, eliciting condemnations from international press freedom and human rights organizations. Farah was arrested for "undermining army morale" and for libel charges stemming from a March 6 article accusing the army leadership of politically motivated dismissals, as well as an April 17 article questioning an army leader's neutrality and alleging misconduct. The state owns and closely controls all domestic broadcast media in addition to *La Nation*, the country's principal newspaper, and coverage favors the government. However, international radio is available, including coverage from the BBC, RFI, VOA, and Radio Sawa, the latter two beginning broadcasts this year. In general, journalists are poorly paid and lack adequate training.

Dominica

LEGAL ENVIRONMENT: 3
POLITICAL ENVIRONMENT: 7
ECONOMIC ENVIRONMENT: 7

Status: Free   TOTAL SCORE: 17

Freedom of the press is unrestricted and media offer a variety of political viewpoints. Journalists operate in a relatively open environment. Four private newspapers compete with four political party journals. There is one state-owned and one independent radio station. Citizens enjoy unrestricted access to the Internet, cable television outlets, and regional radio broadcasts. All media outlets are free to publish without constraint, and all express views opposing government policies; however, the state-owned radio station functions under a government-appointed board that exerts some political influence over content and editorial stances.

Dominican Republic

LEGAL ENVIRONMENT: 8
POLITICAL ENVIRONMENT: 16
ECONOMIC ENVIRONMENT: 15

Status: Partly Free   TOTAL SCORE: 39

Press freedom continued to erode during 2003 as the country's political and economic situation worsened. A major case of bank fraud surfaced in May, further upsetting the economy and disaffecting the public. The collapse of Banco International (Baninter) and the apparent large network of its money-laundering operations, including alleged connections with a wide spectrum of political leaders, caused the authorities to seize the media holdings also owned by the president of Baninter, Ramon Baez

Figueroa. Through the media empire Listin Group, Mr. Baez owned controlling shares in the country's oldest and most prestigious newspaper, the *Listin Diario*, 3 other newspapers, 4 television stations, and 92 radio stations. Authorities immediately fired the editor of *Listin Diario*, replacing him with a former spokesperson for the ministry of agriculture. In protest, the senior editors of the other three newspapers resigned; these three newspapers have since closed due to financial problems. Media advocacy groups allege that the content and orientation of the remaining media have significantly changed, be it through softer headlines and editorials or the slanted endorsement of official policy. Also in 2003, five journalists were interrogated, detained, or publicly accused of defamation by government officials. Another journalist, Julio Gomez, had his car set on fire after a previous attempt by unknown assailants to burn down his house. Gomez, who is a correspondent for several media and radio stations, believes the attacks are connected to his reporting on discrepancies in the government Public Transportation Vehicles Renovation Plan.

East Timor

Status: Free

LEGAL ENVIRONMENT: 6
POLITICAL ENVIRONMENT: 11
ECONOMIC ENVIRONMENT: 12
TOTAL SCORE: 29

Since East Timor's referendum for independence from Indonesia in 1999 and the violent and destructive withdrawal by the Indonesian military that ensued, a fledging press has emerged that contrasts with that under Indonesia's occupation, when independent reporting was not tolerated. Nascent media are supported by a new constitution that provides for freedom of speech and the press, and the government generally respects these rights. Critics note that the constitution makes freedom of expression dependent on several legal provisions, however, and some media experts foresee court battles in the future to settle conflicts raised by press, libel, and broadcast regulation laws. There are two daily newspapers, two weeklies, and a state radio and television station. The broadcast media were handed over to the government by the interim UN administration upon the country's official independence in May 2002, and some express concern that the ruling party (Fretilin) maintains pervasive influence over the station's content. Radio service is available throughout the country, while lack of infrastructure confines television broadcasts to the capital, Dili. A Catholic church radio station also exists, as well as a handful of community radio stations, which are heavily funded by international donors. Insufficient resources constrain development of further print or broadcast media.

Ecuador

Status: Partly Free

LEGAL ENVIRONMENT: 12
POLITICAL ENVIRONMENT: 18
ECONOMIC ENVIRONMENT: 12

TOTAL SCORE: 42

The constitution provides for freedom of speech and press, and the country is usually regarded as enjoying a vigorous press. Independent media exist and actively criticize the government. However, libel and slander are criminal offenses and can be punished by up to three years in prison. There is general recognition that journalists practice self-censorship due to the severe defamation laws and the military's influential position in politics and business. In several cases journalists received various threats, including interrogation by government officials. Former coup leader Lucio Gutierrez took office in January after winning elections in November 2002, and while he promised to fight corruption and social injustice, journalists criticized his administration's aggressive attitude toward the press and the unwillingness of some public agencies and the armed forces to release public information. The daily newspaper *El Comercio* has been pressured by the president to reveal its sources on a story that alleges a connection between $30,000 in drug trafficking money and a donation to the president's campaign in the last election; the newspaper has refused to release any sources on grounds of press freedom. Positively, a Freedom of Information Act passed one round of votes in Congress in September, and appeals related to a libel suit filed against newspaper columnist Rodrigo Fierro have further brought the issue of criminal defamation before the country's Supreme Court of Justice.

Egypt

LEGAL ENVIRONMENT: 26
POLITICAL ENVIRONMENT: 28
ECONOMIC ENVIRONMENT: 22

Status: Not Free   TOTAL SCORE: 76

Although Egyptians have the ability to express their views openly in a diversity of media outlets, press freedom in Egypt continues to suffer from vague laws, uneven implementation of the laws, and control by the government. The Press Law, Publications Law, and penal code regulate and govern the press. The penal code provides for fines and imprisonment for criticisms of the president, members of government, and foreign heads of state. The specific provisions of the law are vague. Although the Supreme Constitutional Court agreed more than five years ago to review the constitutionality of penal code provisions that provide for imprisonment of journalists guilty of libel, the court has yet to issue a ruling on the case. In 2003, the government facilitated a greater diversity of media outlets, with the Shura Council's Higher Council for the Press approving the registration of nearly 40 new magazines and newspapers. The government provides subsidies to most major newspapers, and it owns shares in Egypt's three largest newspapers, whose editors are appointed by the president. Opposition parties have the ability to publish their own newspapers. In July, the ministry of interior banned the distribution of the second issue of the opposition *Al-Saada* newspaper without a court order, and state security officials told the chairman of the paper that the government did not approve of its editorial policy. In September, the government banned the distribution of the London-based *Al-Quds Al-Arabi* newspaper, allegedly because of criticisms of Egypt's president. The government controls content in the state-owned broadcast media. Egypt permitted the establishment of three private satellite television stations, but their owners have close ties to the government. In October, one of these private satellite television stations, Dream TV, canceled a program with a prominent political analyst, Muhammad Hassanein Heikal, after government officials objected to the program's content.

El Salvador

Status: Partly Free

LEGAL ENVIRONMENT: 11
POLITICAL ENVIRONMENT: 17
ECONOMIC ENVIRONMENT: 14
TOTAL SCORE: 42

The press is generally allowed to report openly; freedom of speech and of the press is respected in the constitution. However, strong restrictions on access to information hinder the press, and many journalists and news organizations practice self-censorship to avoid reprisals from the government or big business. The current administration, led by President Francisco Flores Perez and the right-wing National Republican Alliance, is accused of rarely meeting with journalists and then only under strict conditions. Journalists report that media outlets also censor their own news, while media companies complain that government-funded public service announcements are placed in those outlets that are most supportive of government policy. A popular current affairs television program that is often critical of the government, *Sin Censura* (Uncensored), was removed from the air in March after the network's private shareholders bent to the realities of the program's financial difficulties due to an advertising embargo reportedly led by the government and big business interests. Press freedom advocates expressed their frustration that the network had not disclosed to the public the reasons behind the show's departure. Legislation passed in 2002, including a provision in the criminal code that allows judges to close courts and a national audit law that permits public audits to be classified until either they are approved or a lengthy appeals process has been exhausted, have placed further restrictions on press freedom.

Equatorial Guinea

Status: Not Free

LEGAL ENVIRONMENT: 26
POLITICAL ENVIRONMENT: 35
ECONOMIC ENVIRONMENT: 28
TOTAL SCORE: 89

Freedom of expression and of the press is protected under the constitution but the government usually limits the exercise thereof, causing journalists to toil under extremely difficult conditions, with self-censorship a matter of course. Critical coverage of the president or of the security forces often draws reprisals, which range from imprisonment without charge to harassment, beatings, and even forced exile. Police and law enforcement representatives routinely demand bribes of newspaper publishers, threatening to revoke their licenses for imaginary violations of the press laws, and members of the presidential clan are known to harass outspoken journalists. The press corps is noticeably dominated by pro-government opinion-makers; of the half-dozen papers that are published regularly only one, run by the political opposition, is openly critical of authorities. The pervading atmosphere of political censorship has compelled many publications to focus on culture, entertainment, and sports gossip to avoid the government's wrath. With applications for private radio stations pending since the early 1990s, the government dominates the airwaves with the official Radio Malabo; the only existing "private" broadcaster, Radio and Television Asonga, is owned by the president's son, a government minister. The press corps is extremely small, with a grand total of no more than 70 members, who are under legal obligation to register with the ministry of information, which has power de-register journalists and apply government censorship wherever it sees fit. In November, police arrested Agence France-Presse correspondent Rodrigo Angue Nguema for an article on rumored plans for a military coup d'etat. Although the government forcefully denied the report, Nguema was detained without charge for close to two weeks. Three other journalists suffered similar ordeals during the year.

Eritrea

Status: Not Free

LEGAL ENVIRONMENT: 28
POLITICAL ENVIRONMENT: 38
ECONOMIC ENVIRONMENT: 23
TOTAL SCORE: 89

Conditions for the media continued to be severely constrained in 2003. Although freedom of expression is nominally provided for in the constitution, the 1996 press law makes this right subject to the official interpretation of "the objective reality of Eritrea," forbids private ownership of broadcast media, and requires that all newspapers and reporters be licensed. In September 2001, in a dramatic crackdown against independent media and other forms of political dissent, the government banned all privately owned newspapers and arrested at least 10 leading journalists, ostensibly on the grounds of national security. The arrests of other members of the press during 2002 brought the total number of imprisoned journalists to 18 (14 remain detained), according to the Committee to Protect Journalists. After some of the detainees began a hunger strike, they were transferred from prison to unknown places of detention and held incommunicado. At least six journalists have fled abroad, while most foreign correspondents have also left Eritrea as they are unable to operate freely. The arrests continued in 2003: Voice of America stringer Aklilu Solomon was arrested at his home in July and taken to a military camp to complete his mandatory national service (despite a documented medical exemption), a tactic often used by authorities on targeted journalists.

	LEGAL ENVIRONMENT: 6
	POLITICAL ENVIRONMENT: 5
Estonia	ECONOMIC ENVIRONMENT: 6
Status: Free	TOTAL SCORE: 17

The Estonian constitution, adopted in 1992, guarantees freedom of expression and bans censorship. Defamation has not been decriminalized, but no cases were prosecuted in 2003. Although small, the Estonian media market is one of the freest in Eastern Europe. Estonia boasts a wide array of newspapers, magazines, and Internet news portals, although concern has been expressed over the level of foreign investment and control of the media. Since 1998, foreign capital has led to concentration of ownership, especially in print media. Today, foreign investors—primarily Swedish and Norwegian companies such as Bonnier and Schibsted—own 7 of the top 10 newspapers. Estonians enjoy access to Russian, Finnish, and German television, as well as 3 nationwide Estonian stations. While there is little political pressure on media from local authorities, the Russian foreign ministry called on Estonia to shut down the pro-independence Chechen website, KavkazCenter, but the request was rejected. The Estonian news agency Eesti Teadete Agentuuri (ETA) closed in January due to economic difficulties.

	LEGAL ENVIRONMENT: 24
	POLITICAL ENVIRONMENT: 23
Ethiopia	ECONOMIC ENVIRONMENT: 19
Status: Not Free	TOTAL SCORE: 66

While a 1992 law guarantees freedom of the press, the government restricts this right in practice. Throughout 2003, laws concerning publishing false information, inciting ethnic hatred, libel, and publishing articles offensive to public morality were used to justify the arrest, detention, prosecution, and fining of journalists. At least several dozen more journalists have fled the country and live in self-imposed exile rather than face pending court cases. Press freedom organizations and local journalists, led by the Ethiopian Free Press Journalists' Association (EFJA), continued to voice concern with a draft press law and code of ethics presented by the government in 2002, which they feared could be used to restrict the operations of the media further. In November and December, the ministry of justice banned the operation of the EFJA and suspended several executive committee members from their positions, accusing the organization of failing to renew its license and submit audited financial statements to the government. However, EFJA president Kifle Mulat insisted that the EFJA had submitted all the required paperwork, instead alleging that the association was shut down due to its vociferous opposition to the draft press law. While foreign broadcasts are available, domestic broadcast media are state-run, and some journalists practice self-censorship. Although official harassment continues most frequently in the form of legal action, reporters are also subjected to occasional intimidation and physical violence at the hands of police and security forces. At year's end, 35 journalists had cases pending and several continued to be detained under charges filed the previous year. The independent print media remain lively and critical of the government, but most publications are not distributed widely throughout the country. High annual licensing fees and bureaucratic licensing procedures impose additional restraints on newspapers' ability to publish, while reporters continue to face obstacles to gaining access to official information.

Fiji

LEGAL ENVIRONMENT: 6
POLITICAL ENVIRONMENT: 13
ECONOMIC ENVIRONMENT: 10

Status: Free

TOTAL SCORE: 29

Although the constitution provides for freedom of press and speech, the government attempts to exercise considerable authority in restricting these rights. After the 2000 failed coup attempt by businessman George Speight, Fiji's media remain vibrant despite the ongoing political instability. Many members of the local media report that harassment of or attacks on journalists have declined under Prime Minister Laisenia Qarase's administration, although officials do commonly make verbal attacks on the media for exposing political and social problems. The independent Media Council rejected a proposed media bill that would establish further laws and government regulations on the press. It argued that the bill threatens the integrity of press freedom expressed in the constitution and duplicates the regulations currently administered by the council. Although some media are privately owned, the government maintains a television monopoly and holds a stake in several newspapers. Radio is a key source of information; the government operates four stations through the state-owned Fiji Broadcasting Corporation. Several independent radio stations also exist. In a victory for independent media, the Major Tenders Board awarded a public contract of $630,000 to a private radio station in December, upsetting some top government officials. Media objectivity is cited by some as a concern, especially in crisis situations such as the last coup attempt.

Finland

Status: Free

LEGAL ENVIRONMENT: 2
POLITICAL ENVIRONMENT: 2
ECONOMIC ENVIRONMENT: 5
TOTAL SCORE: 9

A new press freedom act, prepared with input from media organizations, was scheduled to enter into force on January 1, 2004. The law was revised to exclude proposed requirements that Internet service providers monitor content. More than 200 newspapers are published in the country, and the printed press is subsidized. Although most newspapers were at one time connected with a political party, more than 90 percent are now officially unaffiliated. In broadcast media, the state runs four of the five national radio stations and two of the four national terrestrial television stations; it has a much less significant presence in cable and satellite television, which are growing. Over the last 10 years, prosecutions and fines have increased for journalists accused of defamation.

LEGAL ENVIRONMENT: 4
POLITICAL ENVIRONMENT: 10

France

ECONOMIC ENVIRONMENT: 5

Status: Free

TOTAL SCORE: 19

The constitution and governing institutions generally maintain a free and open press environment, although a number of violations of press freedom have occurred in recent months. In April 2003, a controversial new internal security bill, known as the Perben law, was introduced that included provisions requiring all persons to hand over any documents requested by authorities; if passed, the bill would threaten the confidentiality of journalists' sources. Police searched the home of journalist Gilles Millet in June as part of an investigation into his possession of confidential material; although the right to freedom of information exists, it can be restricted in such cases to protect the reputation or rights of a third party. Millet was convicted in October and given a suspended sentence. Several accusations were made that the government and/or media owners influence media content, including claims of bias in coverage of the war in Iraq. Journalists covering demonstrations outside the Franco-Africa summit meeting in Paris in February were detained without explanation. The empty car of a journalist who had written on a bomb attack in Corsica was found with bullet holes in September, an occurrence consistent with previous threats to journalists in Corsica. France strictly enforces guidelines requiring 60 percent of broadcast content to be of EU origin. Internet access is unrestricted.

LEGAL ENVIRONMENT: 22
POLITICAL ENVIRONMENT: 20

Gabon

ECONOMIC ENVIRONMENT: 20

Status: Not Free

TOTAL SCORE: 62

Status change explanation: Gabon's status changed from Partly Free to Not Free due to the continued crackdown on the private press and the government's persistent habit of de-licensing private news organizations, as well as an overall countrywide worsening of the free speech environment.

The state-owned *L'Union* is Gabon's leading opinion maker and its only daily newspaper, thanks in large part to a clampdown on the private press orchestrated by the government in clear violation of the constitution, which provides for freedom of the press. Strict licensing requirements and the state's entrenched practice of revoking licenses of news outlets critical of the government continue to inhibit the work of independent journalists. While the government owns and tightly controls the editorial content of two radio stations with countrywide range, the seven privately owned radio stations still allowed to operate remain strictly apolitical. Four private television stations daily transmit eight hours of non-controversial programming, and the state's own two television operations also refrain from criticizing government and ruling party officials. In July, lawmakers scrapped presidential term limits through a constitutional amendment, leaving Omar Bongo, who has been in power since 1968, free to seek reelection for the remainder of his life. While *L'Union* and other pro-government news outlets glossed over the amendment, the beleaguered private press pondered its own and the political opposition's chances of survival in starkly pessimistic terms. Anxious to pacify a resentful private press in the weeks leading to the vote in parliament, the authorities offered financial aid to all news outlets, regardless of editorial stance. The largesse, however, failed to impress independent journalists, most of whom opposed the constitutional amendment. The Conseil National de la Communication (CNC), a government body charged with promoting good journalistic ethics, also failed to allay the media's anxieties. In fact, the CNC this year suspended two private publications, *Le Temps* and *L'Autre Journal*, and banned two others, *La Sagaie* and *Sub-Version*, for "attacking the dignity of the institutions of the Republic."

The Gambia

Status: Not Free

LEGAL ENVIRONMENT: 20
POLITICAL ENVIRONMENT: 25
ECONOMIC ENVIRONMENT: 18
TOTAL SCORE: 63

Although the constitution provides for freedom of expression, the government continues to restrict this right through a combination of harassment and harsh legal strictures. Several decrees require all private media to pay exorbitant licensing fees in order to operate. During 2003, provisions of the National Media Commission Bill of 2002 came into effect. The bill authorized the creation of a commission with the power to decide who is and is not a journalist, to formulate a journalistic code of ethics, and to deny the right to confidentiality of sources. In addition, the commission can issue arrest warrants for journalists and can jail journalists for up to six months on widely framed charges of contempt. The act is currently being challenged in court by the Gambia Press Union. Despite some self-censorship and a lack of access to official information, the independent print media continue to criticize government policies as well as the ruling party. However, the state-run broadcast media present tightly controlled news and give limited coverage to opposition viewpoints. Citizen FM radio, which was an important source of independent news information, was shut down by authorities in 2001 and remained closed during 2003. Journalists continue to experience harassment and attacks at the hands of police and security forces. Staff from the private, biweekly *Independent* were targeted in particular; a reporter was assaulted by police in August, and editor-in-chief Abdoulie Sey was detained incommunicado at the headquarters of the National Intelligence Agency for three days in September. Unidentified men set the newspaper's office on fire in October, but the case has thus far not been adequately investigated.

Georgia

Status: Partly Free

LEGAL ENVIRONMENT: 16
POLITICAL ENVIRONMENT: 23
ECONOMIC ENVIRONMENT: 15
TOTAL SCORE: 54

Freedom of speech and the press is legally protected under the constitution and media legislation, and censorship is prohibited. The country's independent media frequently produce reports critical of the government and conduct investigations into allegations of official corruption. However, the authorities at times have used threats or violence to intimidate journalists investigating corruption and other sensitive subjects, and criminal libel laws encourage some self-censorship. The state has also failed to protect journalists from attack by non-state actors, including followers of the radical defrocked Georgian Orthodox priest, Basili Mkalavishvili. The independent radio station Dzveli Kalaki has been the repeated target of verbal and physical harassment by Mkalavishvili's supporters, who opposed one of the station's programs about Georgia's Catholic minority. The popular independent television station Rustavi-2 has for years endured threats, attacks, and numerous libel lawsuits for reporting on politically sensitive issues such as government corruption. In 2003, the head of the Georgian Railway won a libel suit against the station for information in a program linking him to bribery scandals. In July, a former police officer was sentenced to prison for the 2001 murder of Rustavi-2 journalist Georgi Sanaya. His wife and colleagues maintain that his killing was politically motivated because of his investigations into government corruption and that those who masterminded his murder remain unpunished. Rustavi-2 gave extensive coverage to reports of voter fraud in the November 2003 election and the subsequent mass protests that led to President Eduard Shevardnadze's resignation. The government finances and controls the main television and radio networks, which generally reflect official viewpoints. Independent broadcast media often must depend on local officials and businesspeople for financial support and are subject to their editorial influence. The independent sector dominates the country's press, which struggles financially because of widespread poverty, inadequate advertising revenues, and low circulation. As a consequence, many newspapers are subsidized by and subject to the influence of their patrons in business and politics.

Germany

Status: Free

LEGAL ENVIRONMENT: 5
POLITICAL ENVIRONMENT: 6
ECONOMIC ENVIRONMENT: 5
TOTAL SCORE: 16

The basic law guarantees freedom of expression and of the press, although there are exceptions for hate speech, Holocaust denial, and Nazi propaganda, as well as obscene, violent, or "dangerous" material on the Internet. German privacy laws are sometimes at odds with press freedom. In March, the Constitutional Court authorized police to trace journalists' phone calls in "serious" cases; as "serious" was not defined, this leaves judges to determine whether press freedom should outweigh the fight against crime. The possibility of a federal freedom of information law has been rejected by some regions, thus preventing its passage. After two newspapers published articles early in the year claiming that Chancellor

Gerhard Schroeder was having marital problems, the chancellor sued and a court issued a ban on writing about his private life. The British *Mail on Sunday* was also banned from selling its edition containing the story in Germany. The states oversee public radio and television broadcasters, but there are many private stations as well. The press is dominated by numerous regional papers. However, in the past two decades, financial pressures have consolidated the private media sector, and today a handful of centralized editorial offices control most content, and only a few commercial groups dominate the media market.

Ghana

Status: Free

LEGAL ENVIRONMENT: 9
POLITICAL ENVIRONMENT: 9
ECONOMIC ENVIRONMENT: 10
TOTAL SCORE: 28

Freedom of the press is guaranteed by law and is generally respected in practice. Ghana's diverse and growing media landscape comprises approximately 50 independent and state-run newspapers, 11 government and 60 private radio stations, foreign periodicals and broadcasts, and a number of private and publicly run television stations. Due to the 2001 repeal of the Criminal Libel and Sedition Laws, increased freedom of expression and open criticism of governmental policies and officials appears in both private and government-owned media reports. However, authorities have reportedly pressured state-run media outlets to restrict opposition party coverage. A draft of the Right to Information Bill of the Republic of Ghana was released for public comment in late 2003 and was expected to be submitted to parliament in early 2004. In May, the president replaced the minister of communications with a new appointee as chairman of the National Communications Authority, the body responsible for allocating media licenses, due to complaints that the original appointment represented a conflict of interest. While the number of privately owned media outlets is growing, the weak economic situation stresses their viability, as advertising revenue is limited. Poorly paid journalists may also be susceptible to bribery. In August, a journalist was charged with extortion for threatening to publish an unfavorable article on a government official unless he received money to keep silent.

Greece

LEGAL ENVIRONMENT: 8
POLITICAL ENVIRONMENT: 14
ECONOMIC ENVIRONMENT: 6

Status: Free   TOTAL SCORE: 28

The constitution guarantees freedom of expression. While the government has at times acted to restrict press freedom, media generally enjoy these rights in practice. Libel of the president is a criminal offense but defendants are generally released on bail. The television station Mega Channel was fined for showing two men kissing, which was described by the National Council of Radio and Television as "vulgar and unacceptable." An Albanian journalist who had been in the country since 1991 was denied renewal of his working permit because, authorities said, of "reasons of security and public order." In December 2002 he had written an "open letter" on behalf of all Albanian immigrants. In September an incendiary device was thrown at the front door of a television presenter in Athens, presumably in connection with her investigations into the 17 November terrorist group. The majority of newspapers are privately owned.

Grenada

LEGAL ENVIRONMENT: 6
POLITICAL ENVIRONMENT: 5
ECONOMIC ENVIRONMENT: 5

Status: Free   TOTAL SCORE: 16

Freedom of the press in unrestricted, and the media are free of censorship and government control. Reporters, however, operate cautiously under slander and libel laws, which the state commonly uses to prosecute journalists. A private corporation, with a minority government share, owns the principal radio and television stations. There are 10 active radio stations; at least 4 additional licenses were issued in 2003. There are three public television stations and one cable system. Numerous daily and weekly newspapers routinely carry press releases by opposition parties, including regular weekly columns expressing opposition views. Television stations frequently broadcast reports on opposition activities, including coverage of political rallies held by assorted parties and candidates, public forums featuring political leaders of each of the major parties, and other public service programs. In 2003 the government commenced holding weekly ministerial press conferences in which members of the media are free to ask any questions they wish concerning the relevant ministry.

Guatemala

Status: Not Free

LEGAL ENVIRONMENT: 17
POLITICAL ENVIRONMENT: 30
ECONOMIC ENVIRONMENT: 15

TOTAL SCORE: 62

Status change explanation: Guatemala's status changed from Partly Free to Not Free to reflect increased threats of violence and extralegal intimidation faced by journalists in 2003.

Guatemala's constitution provides for the establishment of a free press. Newspapers maintain their independence by reporting critically on government policies. A Supreme Court decision recently struck down a law requiring journalists to be part of a governmentally licensed union. Yet the fragile state of security throughout Guatemalan society, which emerged in 1996 from decades of civil war, extends especially to journalists who investigate historical occurrences of human rights abuses by former government officials and agencies. Throughout 2003, these investigative journalists faced considerable pressure to curtail their reporting activities, often backed by threats of violence or abduction. The government of President Alfonso Portillo, elected in 1999, continues to be widely accused of gross corruption in attempting to exert influence over the press. Elections held in November sparked a wave of violence and intimidation. The Committee to Protect Journalists described Guatemala in 2003 as "one of the most dangerous places in the Americas to work as a journalist." Four journalists were abducted in October by former paramilitaries, who used the abducted journalists as bargaining chips in order to exact compensation for services they had rendered the government during the recent civil war. In July, a mob of supporters for the government opponent, General Efrain Rios Montt, harassed several members of the press whom they had blamed for a Supreme Court decision that had denied Montt the right to run for president. Hector Ramirez of Radio Sonora, one of the journalists targeted in the attacks, died of a heart attack after being chased by the vigilantes throughout Guatemala City. Many journalists practice self-censorship to avoid these perils. A Mexican media tycoon,

Remigio Angel Gonzalez, owns all of the country's television stations. The stations have been criticized for being monopolistic and too pro-government. The government uses heavy licensing fees to regulate the establishment of new media outlets. News coverage tends to focus on Guatemala City, ignoring the issues of provincial areas and the country's large indigenous population.

Guinea

Status: Not Free

LEGAL ENVIRONMENT: 24
POLITICAL ENVIRONMENT: 29
ECONOMIC ENVIRONMENT: 18
TOTAL SCORE: 71

While Guinea's constitution guarantees freedom of the press, this right is not respected in practice. Restrictive press laws permit the government to censor publications, and defamation and slander are considered criminal offenses. In 2002, Justice Minister Abou Camara attempted to improve press freedom by banning the judicial police from arresting journalists for press offenses. While arrests of journalists declined in 2003, there were numerous reports of journalists' being interrogated and harassed, physically assaulted by the Internal Security Service (DST) and the presidential guard, and suspended as a result of their reporting. Coverage of the December 2003 presidential elections also witnessed numerous abuses of press freedom. The DST summoned and harassed journalists and newspaper editors for articles critical of the president and the legitimacy of the elections. In doing so, the DST violated Guinea's constitution, which specifies that the National Communications Council, the governmental media regulatory body, is the only group authorized to summon and question journalists. Jean Marie Dore, the spokesman for the main alliance of opposition parties, was also arrested and later released for his criticism of President Lansana Conte during a radio interview with Radio France Internationale. While more than a dozen private newspapers are critical of the government, the government controls all radio and television stations and publishes the only daily newspaper. There is little to no coverage of opposition parties in the government-owned media. Although the law does not prohibit licensing private broadcast media, the government denies all applicants on the grounds of national security. High operating costs also contribute to the constraints on private media growth.

Guinea-Bissau

LEGAL ENVIRONMENT: 17
POLITICAL ENVIRONMENT: 27
ECONOMIC ENVIRONMENT: 19

Status: Not Free   TOTAL SCORE: 63

Status change explanation: Guinea-Bissau's rating moved from Partly Free to Not Free to reflect an increase in press freedom violations by the government against both the private and public media in an attempt to silence opposition voices related to the elections.

Constitutional guarantees of freedom of expression and of the press are not well respected in practice. The months leading up to the expected general elections, ending with the coup of September 2003, were characterized by increased government crackdowns on the media. Numerous arrests and acts of official censorship began with the December 2002 banning of the Portuguese station, Radiotelevisao Portuguesa, and the expulsion of its bureau chief amid claims that the station tarnished the image of the country. February 2003 witnessed the closing of the country's main private and opposition radio station, Bombolom FM. A few weeks earlier, Radio Bombolom had broadcast a debate in which Joao Vaz Mane, Vice President of the Guinean Human Rights League, criticized the president. Mane was arrested the next day and detained for three weeks without charge. The government also acted to assault and suspend state-run Radio Difusao Nacional journalist Ensa Seidi for his coverage of former Prime Minister Francisco Fadul's return to Guinea-Bissau to compete in the scheduled elections. Journalists, particularly those in the state-run print and broadcast media, continued to practice self-censorship. A few private newspapers and radio stations are in operation in addition to the government-run weekly newspapers and radio and television stations. Due to financial constraints and government control of the sole printing house, newspapers are published sporadically.

LEGAL ENVIRONMENT: 4
POLITICAL ENVIRONMENT: 8
Guyana
ECONOMIC ENVIRONMENT: 8

Status: Free
TOTAL SCORE: 20

The constitution provides for a free press, and newspapers and television stations are generally able to report without interference. In addition to the state-owned newspaper, the *Guyana Chronicle,* two independent papers, the *Stabroek News* and the *Kaietuer News,* are printed daily, as well as numerous weekly newspapers published by various interest groups. At least 12 independent television stations exist. However, there are no private radio stations, and media advocates such as the Association of Caribbean Media Workers have publicly noted their concern over these restrictions on broadcasting. The government argues that it is unable to issue radio licenses because there is no legislation enabling it to do so. A violent arson attack in January on *Kaietuer News* by two unidentified armed men raised appeals for press freedom from both journalists and the government.

LEGAL ENVIRONMENT: 19
POLITICAL ENVIRONMENT: 39
Haiti
ECONOMIC ENVIRONMENT: 21

Status: Not Free
TOTAL SCORE: 79

Although freedom of expression is protected in the constitution, this right is not upheld. As the political situation deteriorated in late 2003, so did press freedom and the objectivity of the media. Government-run media are biased, and many private media outlets blatantly favor either the government or the opposition. This worsened as violent protests increased toward the end of the year, when a large portion of the independent media openly took the opposition's side. Although some journalists are critical of the government, investigative journalism is rare due to fears of retaliation, and many journalists practice self-censorship. Journalists are frequently harassed by government supporters or physically threatened, and perpetrators are rarely punished. The March results of an inquiry into the 2000 killing of Haiti's best-known journalist, Jean Dominique, focused on those who carried out the murder, all of whom were already in prison, and failed to address much-suspected government involvement.

Many journalists have gone into hiding or fled the country. In February, the owner and reporters of one of Haiti's best independent news radio stations, Radio Haiti Inter, shut down the station and left the country as a result of threats. Other incidents included armed men setting fire to a vehicle in a reporter's garage, a reporter receiving a package with a 12mm cartridge and a threatening letter, and a journalist disappearing for two days before being found naked and bound in a sugar cane field. The vehicle carrying five men who opened fire on the premises of Radio Caraibes in October bore an official license plate, but a government spokesman said the car could have been stolen. Pro-government media were also targeted during the political crisis, including with death threats. Access to print media is severely limited by the very low literacy rate, and few Haitians have televisions. Radio is the most important news medium, with more than 100 stations in the country.

Honduras

Status: Partly Free

LEGAL ENVIRONMENT: 14
POLITICAL ENVIRONMENT: 22
ECONOMIC ENVIRONMENT: 16
TOTAL SCORE: 52

Even though the relationship between the government and media has improved under the presidency of Ricardo Maduro, the country's media still suffer from a climate of corruption, bribery, and politicization. Most media outlets are owned by members of a small business elite with intersecting political interests. The constitution provides for free press and speech, yet there has been consistent pressure by successive governments to control and influence the media. This is primarily done through denying media access to government officials and withholding government advertisements from print media. Investigative journalism is active; however, self-censorship is also practiced to avoid upsetting the economic and political elites. It is also commonly believed that many journalists accept bribes to soften or suppress news content. A 1972 Organic Law of the College of Journalists requires all journalists to hold a university degree in journalism; press freedom advocates contend that this is a violation of freedom of expression. Defamation is punished under Article 345 of the criminal code, although a study by the Inter-American Dialogue reports that this law is not widely abused. Positively, Attorney General Roy Edmundo Medina filed an appeal with the

Supreme Court in October arguing that Article 345 is unconstitutional and should be repealed. Journalist German Antonio Rivas, managing director of television station Corporacion Maya Vision-Canal 7, was shot and killed while parking his car in front of the station in November; an attempt on his life had been made in February. It was the first killing of a journalist in Honduras in 20 years; the police reported that the motive was unclear, although shortly before the February attempt Rivas had made controversial reports on alleged ecological damage inflicted by a private mining company as well as coffee and cattle smuggling at the border with Guatemala.

Hungary

LEGAL ENVIRONMENT: 4
POLITICAL ENVIRONMENT: 8
ECONOMIC ENVIRONMENT: 8

Status: Free

TOTAL SCORE: 20

The constitution provides for freedom of press and the variety of news outlets is evidence of a pluralistic media environment. However, state authorities and contending political interest groups continue their efforts to influence media, especially through public broadcasting. An ongoing debate centers on the allocation of members selected to serve on the National Television and Radio Board (ORTT), the body that regulates the country's media; the former governing party and now the largest opposition group, Fidesz, walked out on two meetings in March in protest at the nominating and election procedures. Public television attracts only about 10 percent of viewers. The six public television and radio stations continue to receive disproportionate funding from state resources, despite nearing bankruptcy several times and a ruling from the Constitutional Court stating that public television should be independent in operations and finance. Hungarians receive information primarily from private TV channels, most of which are foreign owned. The concentration of foreign ownership in the national press is also high; 7 out of 10 national dailies and all local dailies are foreign owned. The successful launch of the private, Hungarian-owned news channel, HIR TV, in 2002 and its marked profit in 2003 challenges the argument that state-supported media are necessary to provide balanced coverage. In October, the notion of freedom of speech was challenged when the Hungarian Television Corporation announced that it would halt the broadcast of a program that had previously aired an interview with a controversial British historian who denies the Holocaust. A rally was held outside the station to re-institute the program; however, at year's end it was still banned.

Iceland

Status: Free

LEGAL ENVIRONMENT: 1
POLITICAL ENVIRONMENT: 3
ECONOMIC ENVIRONMENT: 4
TOTAL SCORE: 8

Iceland has an exceptionally open and free media environment. The constitution and governing institutions provide strong guarantees for freedom of expression. Freedom of information legislation has been in place since 1996. There are three national newspapers as well as a number of local papers; independent and party-affiliated newspapers offer a variety of perspectives. The country has five national television stations, one of which is public. An autonomous board of directors oversees the state broadcasting service. Internet access is open and unrestricted. More than 80 percent of the population accesses the Internet from home.

India

Status: Partly Free

LEGAL ENVIRONMENT: 11
POLITICAL ENVIRONMENT: 17
ECONOMIC ENVIRONMENT: 13
TOTAL SCORE: 41

Although journalists face a number of threats and constraints, Indian media continue to provide diverse and robust coverage and are the freest in South Asia. In recent years, the government has occasionally used the Official Secrets Act (OSA) against the press. Kashmiri journalist Iftikhar Ali Gilani, who was charged under the OSA and detained for seven months in 2002, was released in January 2003 after the military admitted that the case against him had been baseless. A case filed under the OSA in July against reporters from the online news portal Tehelka.com was pending at year's end. Authorities also use other security laws, contempt of court charges, and criminal defamation legislation to curb the media. In the southern state of Tamil Nadu, a journalist was charged and jailed under antiterrorism legislation in April, and in November the state assembly passed a resolution calling for the arrest and imprisonment of six journalists following the publication of an article in a prominent national paper that criticized the state's chief minister. Intimidation and violence by a variety of actors remain a concern; one reporter was killed in September and another was abducted by militants in November. In addition, authorities occasionally beat, detain, or otherwise harass journalists. Conditions are particularly difficult in the insurgency-wracked state of Jammu and Kashmir, where militants routinely issue death threats against media personnel. Unidentified gunmen killed local editor Parvaz Mohammed Sultan in January, and in April a bomb attack on state-owned media outlets in Srinagar left five people dead. Other forms of coercion have also been employed against the Kashmiri media; in February, Reporters Sans Frontieres criticized a decision by the state government to stop placing official advertisements in the independent *Kashmir Observer* newspaper, thus depriving it of an important source of revenue. Faced with such pressures, some journalists practice self-censorship. Nevertheless, the privately owned print media, particularly the national and English-language press, provide diverse coverage and frequently criticize the government. The broadcast media are for the most part in private hands, but the state-controlled All India Radio enjoys a dominant position; its news coverage favors the government.

Indonesia

LEGAL ENVIRONMENT: 19
POLITICAL ENVIRONMENT: 24
ECONOMIC ENVIRONMENT: 12

Status: Partly Free

TOTAL SCORE: 55

Although the constitution contains a general provision for freedom of expression, media freedom remains under threat from the government and other actors. Political and business leaders are increasingly resorting to filing criminal defamation cases against media outlets; several editors were charged and convicted during the year. Almost all of the national broadcast media are owned by firms closely connected to the friends or family of former president Suharto, although the new broadcasting law, if implemented, may help to dilute this concentration of influence by forbidding media cross-ownership. The private print press, while at times shoddy and sensationalist, generally reports aggressively on government policies, corruption, political protests, civil conflict, and other formerly taboo issues. However, some journalists practice self-censorship, and poorly paid reporters are susceptible to bribery. Press freedom in the province of Aceh deteriorated sharply after the military launched a May offensive against the separatist Free Aceh Movement (GAM). Martial law administrators limited the access of foreign journalists to the province and forbade local reporters to print statements from the GAM rebels or stories about military atrocities. One journalist was killed in December during a gun battle between troops and rebels after being kidnapped by the GAM in June. A colleague being held hostage with him remained missing at the end of the year. Journalists throughout Indonesia continue to face intimidation and occasional attacks by police, the security forces, paid thugs, religious extremists, and political activists. The Alliance of Independent Journalists recorded several dozen violent attacks during 2003, in addition to a number of cases of threats and harassment.

Iran

Status: Not Free

LEGAL ENVIRONMENT: 27
POLITICAL ENVIRONMENT: 32
ECONOMIC ENVIRONMENT: 20
TOTAL SCORE: 79

Freedom of the press and of expression continued to suffer in 2003, adversely affected by a renewed crackdown on independent media following a series of anti-regime protests in June. While the constitution provides for press freedom except when published ideas are "contrary to Islamic principles, or are detrimental to public rights," in practice the government severely restricts this right, mostly by way of the Press Law and its associated bodies, the Press Supervisory Board and the Press Court. In spite of this oppressive environment, independent print media are robust and critical of government policies. As a result, since 2000 about 100 newspapers and magazines have been shut down for varying lengths of time, and the circulation of pro-reform newspapers has fallen from a peak of more than 3 million to just over 1 million. In 2003, several reformist newspapers were closed and suspended, including the leading reformist dailies *Hayat-e-No* and *Hamshari*, as well as *Avay-e-koredstan*, the first Kurdish-language newspaper banned in Iran. Many reformist newspapers shuttered by the government have turned to the Internet as a freer medium. Consequently, the government began systematically censoring Internet content for the first time in 2003, setting up a commission dominated by religious hardliners to accomplish this task in January. The government directly controls all broadcast media and succeeded in jamming broadcasts by dissident satellite stations during and following the June demonstrations. Journalists are subjected to harsh prison sentences, exorbitant fines, and even the death penalty for violating vaguely worded laws that, among other offenses, prohibit insulting Islam or criticizing the Islamic revolution and its Supreme Leader. Self-censorship is widely practiced as a result. The Press Court sentenced dozens of journalists, mostly pro-reformists, to prison throughout the year. Iran has the highest number of imprisoned journalists in the Middle East; by year's end, 11 journalists were behind bars in Iranian prisons (down from a peak of 22 in July), according to Reporters Without Borders. In an incident that drew international condemnation, Canadian-Iranian photojournalist Zahra Kazemi was bludgeoned to death in prison in July after being arrested while taking photographs outside Evin Prison in Tehran. After offering conflicting explanations for Kazemi's death, the government buried Kazemi in Iran against the wishes of her family, prompting Canada to withdraw its Iranian ambassador. In October, government officials announced that Kazemi's death was the responsibility of a lone intelligence ministry agent, a conclusion that elicited further condemnation from the press freedom community.

	LEGAL ENVIRONMENT: 22
	POLITICAL ENVIRONMENT: 29
Iraq	ECONOMIC ENVIRONMENT: 15
Status: Not Free	TOTAL SCORE: 66

The ouster of Saddam Hussein's regime in Iraq created historic openings for press freedom in Iraq, but the general lack of law and order, as well as the unclear status of laws regulating the press, contributed to a volatile and uncertain environment for the media in Iraq in 2003. The Coalition Provisional Authority (CPA), the occupation authority in Iraq, issued regulations aimed at setting new standards and processes for press freedom while taking into account the ongoing conflict and unstable environment. The CPA's Order 14, issued in June, prohibits media organizations from broadcasting or publishing information aimed at inciting violence and disorder and advocating for the return of the Baath party. Order 14 declared that the CPA has the authority to close media organizations violating the order's guidelines, and the CPA exercised this authority on at least three occasions in 2003. By year's end, the CPA and the interim Iraqi Governing Council had not set new directives for the interim governing authorities concerning regulation of the media. The announcement of interim ministers in the CPA's Memorandum Number 6 of September 2, 2003, did not include the former position of minister of information. A few international press advocacy and human rights organizations pointed out that despite this new order regulating the media, several draconian laws from Saddam Hussein's rule, including the penal code and the Press and Publications Law, technically remained on the books. The Iraqi Media Network (IMN), established by the CPA in May, dominated domestic television broadcasting, though regional satellite news channels such as Al Jazeera and Al Arabiya attracted a strong following. In November, the CPA banned Al Arabiya from operating in Iraq because it broadcast an audiotape of Saddam Hussein calling for attacks on members of the Iraqi interim governing authority. Hostilities throughout the year claimed the lives of 14 journalists in Iraq, according to Reporters Without Borders. International human rights organizations criticized coalition forces for killing two journalists while reportedly returning hostile fire in early April at the Palestine Hotel in Baghdad and for killing a cameraman in August whose camera soldiers mistook for a weapon. Despite the ongoing violence and uncertainty about the legal and regulatory framework, the removal of Saddam Hussein's regime from power created unprecedented openings for press freedom in Iraq, with the emergence of hundreds of new publications and the opening of Internet cafes.

Ireland

Status: Free

LEGAL ENVIRONMENT: 3
POLITICAL ENVIRONMENT: 7
ECONOMIC ENVIRONMENT: 6
TOTAL SCORE: 16

Government plans to amend the Freedom of Information Law sparked criticism from the media. If adopted, the bill would reduce access to government information and deny the right to appeal when information is not disclosed. Fears are also widespread over government plans to introduce a statutory Press Council to regulate the conduct of the press, which would replace the current self-regulatory model. Ireland's libel laws are widely criticized. One of Ireland's most high-profile and outspoken crime journalists, Paul Williams, was threatened twice in November, allegedly by former paramilitaries. Ireland's state-owned national broadcasting organization, RTE, runs three national TV channels as well as four radio stations; there is only one commercial television station, but most of Ireland can also receive British broadcasts. The press is diverse and independent.

Israel

	LEGAL ENVIRONMENT: 5
	POLITICAL ENVIRONMENT: 14
	ECONOMIC ENVIRONMENT: 9
Status: Free	TOTAL SCORE: 28

The press in Israel is generally able to operate freely. While newspaper and magazine articles on security matters are subject to a military censor, the scope of permissible reporting is wide. Publishing the praise of violence is prohibited under the Counter-terrorism Ordinance, and authorities prohibit expressions of support for groups that call for the destruction of Israel. Editors may appeal a censorship decision to a three-member tribunal that includes two civilians. Arabic-language publications are censored more frequently than are Hebrew-language ones. Newspapers are privately owned and freely criticize government policy. Broadcast media, run both privately and by the state, reflect a broad range of opinion. Tensions between foreign journalists and Israel's Government Press Office (GPO) remained strained in 2003. The GPO, citing security concerns, announced it would establish a new accreditation process for journalists that would include background checks by Israel's domestic security agency, the Shin Bet. The government dropped the plan in the face of pronounced opposition by journalists and press freedom groups. Palestinian journalists, however, continued to encounter difficulty obtaining credentials. In November the government ended a months-long boycott of the British Broadcasting Corporation (BBC). Israel ceased accommodating BBC interview requests and inviting BBC reporters to official briefings after the national broadcaster aired a controversial documentary about Israel's undeclared nuclear weapons program. Israel lifted the ban in November after the BBC issued a commitment to objective Middle East reporting and appointed a special adviser on Middle Eastern affairs. In October, the government forced the pirate radio station Arutz Sheva off the air for operating without a license. The station's broadcasts, supportive of Jewish settlers in the West Bank and Gaza, originated from a boat in the

Mediterranean Sea. In November, the Israeli High Court upheld an appeal against a decision by the Israel Film Board to ban the screening of a documentary film critical of Israel's armed forces. [The rating for Israel reflects the state of press freedom within Israel proper, not in the West Bank and Gaza Strip, which is covered in the following report on the Israeli-administered Territories/Palestinian Authority.]

Israeli-Administered Territories/ Palestinian Authority

LEGAL ENVIRONMENT: 29
POLITICAL ENVIRONMENT: 37
ECONOMIC ENVIRONMENT: 20

Status: Not Free   TOTAL SCORE: 86

While journalists continue to cover events in the West Bank and Gaza Strip, international press freedom groups criticized Israel in 2003 for refusing journalists access to conflict zones and for harassing, and in some cases shooting, reporters. In April, Israeli troops shot and killed Nazih Darwazeh, an Associated Press Television News cameraman filming clashes in the West Bank city of Nablus. In May, James Miller, a British cameraman, was shot in apparent crossfire between Israeli Defense Forces (IDF) troops and Palestinian gunmen in Gaza, and later died of his injuries. He was filming a documentary about arms smuggling in the Rafah refugee camp. The same month, British photojournalist Tom Hurndall was shot in the head by IDF troops as they battled gunmen in the West Bank. In June the International Press Institute released its annual "Intifadah Report," which stated that from September 2000 through May 2003, Israelis were responsible for 82.9 percent of the 310 recorded press freedom violations in the West Bank and Gaza Strip. The figures included 10 people killed and 116 injured. The IDF denied that it targeted journalists, saying that reporters covering dangerous clashes risk being harmed unintentionally. In January, the IDF closed two TV stations and one radio station in Hebron during anti-terror operations; since September 2000, the IDF has targeted Palestinian media that spread propaganda and incite violence.

Under a 1995 Palestinian press law, journalists may be fined and jailed and newspapers closed for publishing "secret information" on Palestinian security forces or news that might harm national unity or incite violence. However, another press law, also signed in 1995, stipulates that Palestinian intelligence services do not reserve the right to interrogate, detain, or arrest journalists on the basis of their work. Nevertheless, arbitrary arrests, threats, and the physical abuse of journalists critical of the Palestinian Authority (PA) are routine. Official Palestinian radio and television are government mouthpieces. Journalists covering the Israeli-Palestinian conflict and Palestinian political affairs face harassment by the PA. Officials have threatened journalists who file stories deemed unfavorable. PA-affiliated militias have also warned Israeli journalists to stay out of Palestinian areas. International press freedom groups have called on the PA to cease harassment of journalists. In January, Palestinian intelligence agents raided Al Jazeera TV's Gaza bureau without a warrant, detaining a correspondent. In September, five armed men saying they were members of Al Aqsa Martyrs Brigade raided the Arabiya satellite TV bureau in Ramallah, smashing equipment and threatening to kill workers. The station had received threats over what was perceived to be biased reporting in favor of Israel.

Italy

Status: Partly Free

Legal Environment: 11
Political Environment: 13
Economic Environment: 9
Total Score: 33

Status change explanation: Italy's rating moved downward from Free to Partly Free as a result of high media concentration and increased political pressures on media outlets.

The country's free and independent media institutions are threatened by government interference and the highest level of media concentration in Europe. This trend results from the 20-year failure of political administrations to reform the framework for independent journalism and access to information. In 2003, in response to calls for reform, legislators introduced the controversial so-called Gasparri law, which would have allowed increased cross-ownership of broadcast and print media. Critics asserted, however, that the bill was tailor-made to circumvent a court decision unfavorable to Prime Minister Silvio Berlusconi's media empire, reversing a ruling that would have forced Berlusconi's company to convert its station, Rete 4, to less-profitable satellite television. The bill was approved by parliament but vetoed by

President Carlo Ciampi in December. In response, Berlusconi signed a decree allowing Rete 4 to continue terrestrial broadcasting until April 2004. Claims of government interference in reporting have increased. For example, some journalists complained that coverage of Berlusconi's controversial comments to the European Parliament in July had been deliberately "softened and cut." The editor of *Corriere della Sera,* the major daily, resigned in May amid allegations that he was pressured to quit due to his tense relations with government officials. A journalist in Sicily was attacked by unidentified men in August after publishing articles about local drug trafficking, and shots were fired at the home of a journalist in Sardinia who also appeared to be targeted because of his work. Berlusconi's substantial family business holdings control the three largest private television stations and one newspaper, as well as a significant portion of the advertising market. As prime minister, he is able to exert influence over public-service broadcaster RAI as well, a conflict of interest that is one of the most flagrant in the world. However, the concentration is considerably less in the print media, which continue to be critical of the government.

Jamaica

LEGAL ENVIRONMENT: 4
POLITICAL ENVIRONMENT: 7
ECONOMIC ENVIRONMENT: 6

Status: Free   TOTAL SCORE: 17

A high degree of media independence prevails; the current government, led by the People's National Party and Prime Minister P.J. Patterson, is recognized for its positive stance on press freedom. The four largest newspapers are all privately owned. There are 3 television stations and 16 radio stations. Jamaica has an estimated 1.9 million radios—the highest per-capita ratio in the Caribbean. Efforts to reform press and media legislation center on the country's libel laws, which allow for high damage awards in defamation cases. The newspaper firm Gleaner Company Limited is currently appealing a 1996 libel suit decision against it, which awarded $1,000,000 to the former Jamaican minister of tourism, to the Inter-American Commission on Human Rights.

LEGAL ENVIRONMENT: 3
POLITICAL ENVIRONMENT: 9
Japan
ECONOMIC ENVIRONMENT: 6

Status: Free   TOTAL SCORE: 18

Press freedom is provided for in the constitution and is upheld by an independent judiciary and a functioning democratic political system. However, although the press is free, it is not always outspoken. The European Union has formally complained about the exclusive access to news sources that major media outlets enjoy as members of Japan's 800 or more *kisha* clubs (private press clubs). As club members, these media receive exclusive information from government ministries, political parties, and private firms that is often unavailable to freelancers or to reporters from foreign or small publications, who are barred from some clubs. Journalists who belong to the clubs generally do not report aggressively on the conditions of ailing companies and other sensitive financial issues. Violence against journalists is rare. Nevertheless, in September, the bound and gagged body of freelance journalist Satoru Someya, who was noted for his investigative reporting on organized crime, was found in Tokyo Bay.

LEGAL ENVIRONMENT: 23
POLITICAL ENVIRONMENT: 22
Jordan
ECONOMIC ENVIRONMENT: 18

Status: Not Free   TOTAL SCORE: 63

Jordan took limited steps toward advancing press freedom in 2003 by eliminating elements of the penal code that restricted press freedom and replacing the ministry of information with an appointed Higher Media Council in October. In April, the government repealed Article 150 of the penal code, an amendment introduced by royal decree two years earlier that gave the State Security Court (SSC) the power to close publications and imprison individuals for publishing information deemed harmful to national unity or the reputation of the state. Despite this improvement, other articles of the penal code continue to limit press freedom, such as provisions that restrict criticism of the royal family, the national assembly, and public officials. Prior to the repeal of Article 150, the SSC prosecuted and convicted three journalists from the weekly *Al-Hilal* in February for publishing an article that allegedly demonstrated a lack of respect for the

Prophet Muhammad's family. The government closely monitors content in the print media and enjoys a monopoly on the domestic broadcast media. In August, the government withdrew accreditation for the Qatar-based regional satellite channel, Al-Jazeera, accusing the channel of insulting Jordan's royal family. Informers in newspapers reportedly alert government officials about draft articles and stories that might be considered objectionable, and editors and journalists report pressure from state officials to stop the publication of certain articles. In September 2003, the government ordered the independent weekly *Al-Wehda* to remove an article about torture in Jordanian prisons. When this article was not removed, the government ordered a ban on that edition of the newspaper. Jordanians generally enjoy unrestricted access to the Internet, which is not censored by the government.

Kazakhstan

LEGAL ENVIRONMENT: 25
POLITICAL ENVIRONMENT: 27
ECONOMIC ENVIRONMENT: 22

Status: Not Free

TOTAL SCORE: 74

Freedom of the press remained weak in 2003 following President Nursultan Nazarbayev's crackdown on opposition media in the previous year. Legislation criminalizing the impugning of the "honor and dignity" of the president remains in effect, as does the 1999 Law on Confidential State Affairs, which classifies the economic interests of the president and his family as state secrets. Perhaps in response to international criticism of the lack of press freedom in Kazakhstan, the government proposed a new media law, which it claimed would bring about positive change to the country's media environment. However, the draft law, Concerning Mass Media, which was passed by the lower house of parliament on December 25, 2003, was widely criticized by both national and international media organizations as a tool to restrict media freedom even further. In particular, vaguely worded language that would subject journalists to prison sentences and fines for "propaganda" or revealing undefined state secrets and provisions to shut down media outlets for violation of various articles in the draft law, as well as requirements on independent broadcasters to transmit official government statements, all leave the draft media law in direct contradiction to international standards of press freedom. The continued imprisonment of journalist and human rights activist Sergei

Duvanov for the alleged rape of a minor continued to pose serious questions about press freedom in Kazakhstan. While Duvanov was finally allowed to leave prison following a December 29 court ruling that reduced his sentence, the irregular investigation and flawed trial that had led to his conviction following the publication of an article critical of the president provided a poignant reminder of the risks facing investigative journalists. Threats and physical attacks on reporters remain common, as does self-censorship by journalists and editors. The government controls or influences most newspapers, printing and distribution facilities, and electronic broadcasts. It also categorizes Web sites based in the country as media outlets and periodically blocks access to several opposition sites.

Kenya

Status: Partly Free

LEGAL ENVIRONMENT: 20
POLITICAL ENVIRONMENT: 21
ECONOMIC ENVIRONMENT: 19
TOTAL SCORE: 60

Status change explanation: Kenya's status improved from Not Free to Partly Free because the number of press freedom abuses has decreased and the media generally enjoy greater editorial freedom under a new government elected in December 2002.

The constitution provides for freedom of expression and of the press; the media are very active, but the government sometimes restricts the rights of journalists under sections of the penal code, the Official Secrets Act, the Book and Newspapers Act, or colonial-era libel laws. Security forces often harass, beat, or detain members of the press, but the number of such incidents has decreased in recent years. Under the Media Bill approved by parliament in May 2002, publishers are required to purchase a costly bond before printing and publishing. The law also criminalizes the sale or distribution of print media products not deposited with a registrar within two weeks of publication. Violators face hefty fines or up to six months in prison. In addition, the constitution empowers the government to limit media coverage of debates on issues under consideration by the courts. In 2003, the government repeatedly invoked this particular provision to intimidate journalists who reported on the murder of Crispin Odhiambo Mbai, who headed a key committee of the Constitutional Review Conference. Some public officials threatened libel lawsuits against publications deemed too critical of their conduct or of government decisions. During the year, at least four journalists from leading publications were detained and interrogated because of their work. While print media enjoy greater freedom than in previous years, the state-owned Kenya Broadcasting Corporation remains the only broadcaster with countrywide coverage. The range of the dozen private radio and television stations does not extend beyond the capital, Nairobi. Meanwhile, some 120 applications for radio and television licenses are pending before the government-controlled Communication Commission of Kenya—which has power to issue, withhold, and revoke broadcast licenses—and the backlog is growing as prospective broadcasters continue to apply. Tensions arose between the government and some newspaper publishers in December after the attorney general disclosed plans to outlaw "gutter" periodicals from the expansive tabloid press, which has been accused of politically motivated character assassination through unfounded and exaggerated stories. Independent journalists, who played a crucial role in the December 2002 election of Mwai Kibaki to the presidency, were reluctant to support the government's latest media policies.

Kiribati

Status: Free

LEGAL ENVIRONMENT: 5
POLITICAL ENVIRONMENT: 8
ECONOMIC ENVIRONMENT: 14
TOTAL SCORE: 27

Freedom of press is provided for in the constitution; the government generally respects this right despite an October 2002 amendment to the Newspaper Registration Act, which permits authorities to de-register a newspaper if it "offends" the public or is likely to lead to "disorder." To date, no publications have been de-registered. In December 2002, a former president was finally granted a license to operate the only private radio station, after the government had blocked this request in 1999. The former president also owns the only private newspaper. The government publishes two newspapers and controls two radio stations. Church-published newsletters also serve as important sources of information.

Kuwait

LEGAL ENVIRONMENT: 19
POLITICAL ENVIRONMENT: 22
ECONOMIC ENVIRONMENT: 16

Status: Partly Free

TOTAL SCORE: 57

The constitution provides for freedom of the press, and the media are free to scrutinize the government with some important exceptions. The Printing and Publications Law and the penal code restrict criticism of the emir and of relations with other states; material deemed offensive to religion; and incitements to violence, hatred, or dissent. Journalists who defame Islam are subject to prison sentences. These laws are arbitrarily enforced, and as a result, many journalists practice self-censorship. In June, the government charged Mohammed Jassem, editor of *Al-Watan* newspaper and an advocate for political reform, with challenging the authority of the emir and "uttering abusive statements" about the emir. In May, the government presented a new draft press law that contained some severe restrictions on press freedom, including prepublication censorship; at year's end, the National Assembly had yet to vote on it. The print media are privately owned and independent, but publishers must register with the ministry of information. Broadcast media are government owned. However, access to foreign satellite stations is legal and widespread. Kuwaitis can use the Internet, though Internet service providers have blocked access to certain sites. Journalists are subject to occasional harassment and physical violence. Non-embedded journalists who attempted to cross the Kuwaiti border into Iraq during the U.S.-led invasion of that country were often rebuked by Kuwaiti authorities. Also during the war, the information ministry threatened foreign journalists based in Kuwait with criminal penalties if they filed stories for Israeli media.

Kyrgyzstan

LEGAL ENVIRONMENT: 23
POLITICAL ENVIRONMENT: 27
ECONOMIC ENVIRONMENT: 21

Status: Not Free

TOTAL SCORE: 71

Freedom of expression and of the press is guaranteed by Articles 15 and 16 of Kyrgyzstan's constitution. Nonetheless, press freedom was severely curtailed in 2003, both through a number of government libel lawsuits and through physical attacks against journalists. The end of the year, however, did register bright spots on the media scene as the media community welcomed the opening of the country's first full-service independent printing press in November and as the parliament began debating legislation in December that would introduce a fee on lawsuits filed against the media and decriminalize libel. The law decriminalizing libel, if passed, would require defamation cases to be tried in civil courts. However, many local journalists and international observers remain skeptical that it would reduce government influence over the independent media, as financial pressure would remain an effective tool for stifling critical voices. A number of lawsuits were filed against independent media outlets in 2003. The independent newspaper *Moya Stolitsa* was particularly hard hit. The newspaper, which has been critical of the government and has conducted investigative reports on corruption, has been named as defendant in 34 lawsuits since November 2002. It had received judgments against it amounting to almost $100,000, causing it to close in early summer of 2003. However, it shortly reopened under the new name of *MSN*. *Kyrgyz Ordo*, a Kyrgyz-language paper, also closed down due to the financial burden resulting from court judgments. Government subsidies to a number of print, radio, and television outlets afford them a distinct advantage in competing for advertising revenue. Authorities in the state-controlled distribution system favor state-owned or -controlled press, delaying and often simply refusing to pay independent publishers for copies distributed and sold. In addition to economic pressures, journalists critical of the government faced continued physical harassment. In January, a *Moya Stolitsa* reporter was assaulted, while the car of another journalist from that paper was set on fire. In September the body of investigative journalist Ernis Nazalov was found floating in a canal, and in October an Osh-based reporter was attacked by two assailants. Internet media remained free from legal restrictions and have proven an effective means of transmitting news, although access to the Internet is limited outside Bishkek.

Laos

LEGAL ENVIRONMENT: 28
POLITICAL ENVIRONMENT: 31
ECONOMIC ENVIRONMENT: 23

Status: Not Free

TOTAL SCORE: 82

Laotian media remain tightly controlled by the authoritarian, one-party state. Although the constitution provides for press freedom, that freedom is severely restricted in practice. Sections of the penal code broadly forbid inciting disorder, slandering the state, distorting state policies, or disseminating information or opinions that weaken the state. Foreign journalists must apply for special visas and are restricted in their activities; foreign news reports appearing in Lao publications are subject to censorship. Two European journalists covering the Hmong insurgency and their American interpreter, arrested in June and sentenced to 15-year prison terms, were released in July following considerable international pressure. However, two Hmong assistants arrested with them remain imprisoned under long sentences. The government owns all newspapers and broadcast media, tightly controlling their content. According to Reporters Sans Frontieres, all journalists are employees of the ministry of information and culture and are trained to report information in a way that is "favorable to the government." Authorities also control all domestic Internet servers, sporadically monitoring e-mail and blocking access to some political Web sites.

Latvia

Status: Free

LEGAL ENVIRONMENT: 7
POLITICAL ENVIRONMENT: 4
ECONOMIC ENVIRONMENT: 6

TOTAL SCORE: 17

Latvian media generally operate freely, as guaranteed by the 1991 press law. However, libel and incitement of racial hatred are crimes that carry possible prison sentences of up to three years. More than 200 privately owned newspapers represent a wide range of political views. The majority of television and radio broadcasters are also in private hands. On June 6, 2003, the constitutional court struck down restrictions on the use of Russian and other foreign languages in broadcast media, opening the door for a wide array of foreign and domestic news sources. In an attempt to encourage control of campaign financing, Transparency International-Latvia has proposed placing spending limits on political advertising, but Latvian State Television, along with a coalition of private broadcasters, maintains that the proposal violates democratic principles. An investigation of the 2001 murder of Gundars Matiss, a journalist for the newspaper *Kurzemes Vards*, concluded in July that Matiss was killed in retaliation for his investigative reporting on organized crime. Court proceedings are currently underway against a company indirectly owned by the government to prevent the implementation of a digital television contract that would hinder the ability of private television stations to compete. Use of the Internet in Latvia is unrestricted.

Lebanon

Status: Not Free

LEGAL ENVIRONMENT: 23
POLITICAL ENVIRONMENT: 27
ECONOMIC ENVIRONMENT: 16

TOTAL SCORE: 66

Syria's ongoing dominance of Lebanese politics, government, and society continued to inhibit press freedom in Lebanon in 2003. Although the constitution provides for freedom of the press, Lebanese government actions severely limit this freedom. A 1991 treaty between Syria and Lebanon includes an explicit pledge by Lebanon to ban all political and media activity that might harm Syria; strict defamation and security laws prohibit criticism of top leaders and restrict political debate. In February 2003, Adonis Akra, a professor who wrote a book about his experience in detention after a crackdown on anti-Syrian activists, was indicted on charges of tarnishing the reputation of the judiciary and harming relations with Syria. Amer Mashmoushi, the managing editor of the daily *Al-Liwa*, was indicted in July on charges of defaming the president after writing an article critical of the president's handling of a banking scandal. In December, the Lebanese government temporarily detained Tahsin Khayyat, chairman of the NTV television station, accused him of having ties with Israel and damaging Lebanon's relations with Syria, and banned NTV broadcasts for a two-day period. The 2002 closure of the Murr television station for broadcasting anti-Syria material remained in effect throughout the year, despite legal appeals. A limited degree of diversity and economic freedom does exist in Lebanon's media. Most media outlets in Lebanon are privately owned, including six independent television stations and nearly three dozen independent radio stations. Access to the Internet is generally not restricted.

Lesotho

LEGAL ENVIRONMENT: 11
POLITICAL ENVIRONMENT: 15
ECONOMIC ENVIRONMENT: 14

Status: Partly Free   TOTAL SCORE: 40

The government generally respects freedom of speech and the press, which is provided for in the constitution. A 1938 proclamation prohibits criticism of the government and contains penalties for seditious libel. Defamation lawsuits regularly target journalists and media organizations. In a victory for press freedom, February saw the High Court rule in favor of the independent newspaper *MoAfrika* after the newspaper's editor was summoned to court to defend the content of a recurring announcement in the Sesotho weekly. In July, the financial burden of a penalty resulting from a 1999 defamation lawsuit brought *MoAfrika Radio* to the brink of closure. The government's recently coercive approach to collecting the fine, as well as the disproportionate size of the fine itself, have led to condemnations from press freedom organizations. Several independent newspapers, including two Christian publications and four English-language weeklies, freely criticize the government. State-owned print and broadcast media reflect the views of the ruling party, failing to give equal coverage to opposition parties. Journalists reportedly have trouble gaining access to official information, most recently concerning the treatment of convicted mutineer Katleho Malataliana. Media development remains constrained by under-funding and a lack of resources.

Liberia

LEGAL ENVIRONMENT: 19
POLITICAL ENVIRONMENT: 33
ECONOMIC ENVIRONMENT: 23

Status: Not Free   TOTAL SCORE: 75

Press freedom reached its 2003 low point in July when fighting between government and rebel forces shut down virtually all independent media outlets. However, conditions improved once President Charles Taylor was ousted in August. The transitional government that took power in October promised greater freedom for the press. Liberia's constitution guarantees freedoms of speech and the press, but these rights have not been respected in practice. In June, the director of the National Communication Bureau closed six amateur FM radio stations saying that their "motives and scopes of operations" were "not clear." The government had reportedly previously authorized the stations to operate. Taylor's ministry of information required publications to register with the government annually and had used this power to close antigovernment publications in past years. In October the transition government's new minister of information announced that the requirement would be relaxed. Physical threats from government and antigovernment forces, censorship, and President Taylor's near monopoly on broadcast coverage outside the capital severely restricted independent media coverage as the country's civil conflict intensified in 2003. In June, a reporter from *The News* went into hiding after being attacked and robbed by armed men wearing the uniform of President Taylor's Anti-Terrorist Unit. In July, a French photojournalist was seriously wounded during fighting between government and rebel forces. As fighting increased, the Taylor government ordered all Liberian media outlets to clear stories on the rebellion with the ministry of information prior to publication or broadcast. With Taylor's ouster, independent newspapers began reappearing in the capital and the three-year-old ban on the popular independent station Star Radio was lifted. Conditions for journalists remained dangerous outside Monrovia at year's end. Media outlets face difficulty recovering from economic damage suffered during the conflict. Several media outlets, including Talking Drum Studios and Radio Veritas, were looted or damaged during the fighting, losing tens of thousands of dollars' worth of valuable equipment.

Libya

Status: Not Free

LEGAL ENVIRONMENT: 29
POLITICAL ENVIRONMENT: 36
ECONOMIC ENVIRONMENT: 29
TOTAL SCORE: 94

The extreme restrictions on press freedom in Libya are unparalleled almost anywhere else in the world. Without democratic institutions, an independent judiciary, and political parties, there is no infrastructure to support voices that offer alternatives to the government line. The government owns and controls all media and prohibits discussion of a wide range of topics including criticism of Muammar al-Qadhafi and government policies. In October the official daily, *Al-Zaf Al-Akhdar*, was temporarily shut down after criticizing two other Arab states. Censorship is pervasive and effective. Vague laws restricting freedom of speech, strict licensing of journalists and publications, and an established system of informants has created an atmosphere of fear and mistrust such that few journalists dare to speak out. Telephones are tapped and academic speech is tightly controlled. Although foreign media are available, content is highly monitored and their sale or distribution is often prohibited. Despite the highly controversial nomination of Libya to chair the 2003 UN Human Rights Commission and the subsequent protest by and suspension of Reporters Sans Frontieres from that year's meeting, there may be reason for cautious optimism in the year to come. While domestic print and broadcast media are severely restricted, the Internet remains relatively free. Furthermore, following Qadhafi's landmark decision to dismantle weapons of mass destruction in December, his son Saif al-Islam Quaddaif was quoted saying that the government may follow this decision by allowing more political rights and greater press freedom.

Liechtenstein

Status: Free

LEGAL ENVIRONMENT: 2
POLITICAL ENVIRONMENT: 3
ECONOMIC ENVIRONMENT: 7
TOTAL SCORE: 12

Liechtenstein remains one of the freest media environments in the world. During 2003 no violations of press freedom were reported. Article 40 of the constitution guarantees freedom of expression and the press. Due to the country's small size and location, media of all forms from neighboring Switzerland, Austria, and Germany are widespread. The principality's two daily newspapers, *Liechtensteiner Vaterland* and *Liechtensteiner Volksblatt*, generally reflect the views of the two main political parties. The main radio station, *Radio Liechtenstein*, was privately owned. However, due to the withdrawal of the private sponsor, the government will take over ownership at the beginning of 2004. There are two television stations, a private one and the state broadcaster. Internet access is open and unrestricted.

Lithuania

Status: Free

LEGAL ENVIRONMENT: 5
POLITICAL ENVIRONMENT: 7
ECONOMIC ENVIRONMENT: 6
TOTAL SCORE: 18

As freedom of expression is guaranteed by Article 25 of Lithuania's constitution, journalists are generally able to work without censorship.

However, an ongoing case of harassment by state authorities against the independent daily newspaper *Respublika* calls into doubt government respect for press freedom. Soon after the January 2003 presidential elections, *Respublika* reported that state security forces had been instructed to use any means necessary to silence the press before the 2004 parliamentary elections. When the government responded with an investigation of the daily by tax authorities, evidence emerged that state security services are under orders to monitor *Respublika*. Libel remains a crime in Lithuania, and judicial authorities may order a journalist to reveal confidential sources if such disclosure is necessary to protect other constitutional values. In March, the head of Lithuania's public television network resigned in protest against constant pressure from a small but prominent group of government officials. Access to the Internet is generally unrestricted, although in June state security forces seized the server of the pro-Chechen independence Web site Kavkaz-Center, apparently at the insistence of the Russian government. In September, the Second District Court at Vilnius ruled that the security service had overstepped its authority and ordered the return of the server. However, the court also stated that the site must remove certain material that promoted national and religious hatred, which is prohibited by Lithuanian law.

Luxembourg

LEGAL ENVIRONMENT: 2
POLITICAL ENVIRONMENT: 3
ECONOMIC ENVIRONMENT: 7

Status: Free

TOTAL SCORE: 12

The government has a very liberal media policy, which has helped the country serve as a provider of broadcast services for pan-European audiences. This role has decreased as other countries have liberalized their media markets, thus leaving Luxembourg with less revenue for its small domestic market. Newspapers and magazines present a diverse spectrum of viewpoints, but financial viability depends on support from political parties and trade unions. The government subsidizes media heavily to prevent closures, and many broadcasters operate only for a few hours a day. Government-run media outlets are minor; RTL, a locally-owned media conglomerate dominates the broadcast media.

LEGAL ENVIRONMENT: 17

POLITICAL ENVIRONMENT: 21

Macedonia
ECONOMIC ENVIRONMENT: 15

Status: Partly Free TOTAL SCORE: 53

Although freedom of the press is guaranteed by Article 16 of the constitution, media outlets are under strong political influence from both the ruling party and the opposition, especially through abuse of the legal system, the selective distribution of advertising, and denial of access to information. Nevertheless, the government has made significant progress in drafting and adopting a Law on Freedom of Information. At the same time, however, amendments to the criminal code passed in fall 2003 further restricted freedom of the press. These legislative changes failed to alter the criminal characterization of offenses such as slander and libel. In response to criticism from the Association of Print Media, the parliament declined a request for state funding from the state-owned news agency, Macedonia Information Agency. The Macedonian press also faces a new challenge of industry consolidation. In July, the German media group Westdeutsche Allgemeine Zeitung announced that it had bought three major Macedonian dailies: *Dnevnik, Utrinski Vesnik,* and *Vest,* and incorporated the three newspapers into the new company Media Print Macedonia. With an average circulation of 120,000—and a much larger audience due to readers' common practice of sharing copies—the new conglomerate dominates the market, as the other major newspapers (*Nova Macedonia* and *Vecer)* are considered to have much smaller circulation and investment capabilities. Attacks on journalists and media offices in 2003 declined relative to the previous year; however, several incidents were reported, including a police raid on the Albanian newsroom of public broadcaster MTV in April and an attack on three TV crews by villagers in Aracinovo in June.

LEGAL ENVIRONMENT: 11

POLITICAL ENVIRONMENT: 18

Madagascar
ECONOMIC ENVIRONMENT: 12

Status: Partly Free TOTAL SCORE: 41

Freedom of speech and of the press is enshrined in the constitution; however, the government limits these rights in practice. Defamation is a criminal offense, and journalists are occasionally prosecuted under these laws. A number of daily and weekly newspapers publish material critical of the government and other parties and politicians. Authorities do occasionally pressure media outlets to curb their coverage of certain issues (particularly at the local level), opposition politicians are rarely given access to state-run media, and some journalists practice self-censorship. Although nationwide radio and television broadcasting remain a state monopoly, numerous local, privately owned stations operate across the country. According to the US State Department, journalists report being threatened with physical violence or prosecution by both governmental and societal actors. Journalists, who are paid very poorly, are occasionally bribed by government officials or private companies to assure favorable coverage.

Malawi

Status: Partly Free

LEGAL ENVIRONMENT: 15
POLITICAL ENVIRONMENT: 22
ECONOMIC ENVIRONMENT: 15
TOTAL SCORE: 52

Freedom of speech and of the press is legally guaranteed and generally respected in practice. While 2003 saw some positive developments for press freedom in Malawi, the independent media faced continued restrictions and harassment at the hands of the government and its supporters. Charges of defamation and of offenses under other restrictive laws have been used to prosecute members of the press, resulting in the practice of self-censorship by some journalists. Initially arrested on allegations of publishing information likely to cause a "breach of public peace," in October 2003 *Daily Times* reporter Frank Namangale was cleared of all charges by the Director of Public Prosecution, who subsequently ordered the police to cease their arbitrary arrest of journalists. Although a broad spectrum of opinion is presented in some two dozen private newspapers, the state-owned Malawi Broadcasting Corporation controls television and most radio service; their coverage favors the ruling party. Private radio is often restricted. In June, the government ordered that community radio stations stop broadcasting news bulletins, and Capital Radio was threatened in September with a shutdown for violating the provisions of its license by airing "outside broadcasts." Reporters and media outlets faced verbal threats as well as physical attacks at the hands of police, senior politicians, and supporters of the ruling party throughout the year.

Malaysia

Status: Not Free

Legal Environment: 26
Political Environment: 25
Economic Environment: 18
Total Score: 69

The Malaysian media continued to be sharply constrained by legal restrictions and other forms of intimidation during 2003. The constitution permits limitations on freedom of expression, and the government imposes them in practice, ostensibly to protect national security and public order. The Printing Presses and Publications Act (PPPA) requires all publishers and printing firms to obtain an annual permit to operate, which can be withdrawn without judicial review. Authorities have shut down or otherwise circumscribed the distribution of some pro-opposition media outlets under the PPPA. The Official Secrets Act, Sedition Act, Broadcasting Act, and criminal defamation laws also impose wide restrictions on the press and on other critical voices. Political parties and business people or companies close to the ruling coalition own or control most major newspapers, and political news coverage and editorials strongly support the government line. Similarly, state-run Radio Television Malaysia and the two private television stations offer flattering coverage of the government and rarely air opposition views. Pressure from owners, as well as fear of legal reprisals, encourages many journalists to practice self-censorship. In November, the editor of a major daily was sacked after he wrote an article that called for reform in Saudi Arabia. Foreign publications are subject to censorship, and issues containing critical articles are frequently delayed. Some diversity of opinion is provided in the online editions of newspapers (which are not bound by the PPPA regulations noted above) as well as other independent news Web sites. However, during the year the government engaged in ongoing harassment of the online daily *Malaysiakini.com*. In January, police acting on a complaint from the youth wing of the ruling party raided the Web site's office, interrogated journalists, and confiscated office equipment. The threat of prosecution on sedition charges hung over the Web site at year's end.

LEGAL ENVIRONMENT: 23
POLITICAL ENVIRONMENT: 23

Maldives
ECONOMIC ENVIRONMENT: 18

Status: Not Free   TOTAL SCORE: 64

Press freedom is not provided for by law and is generally not respected in practice. The penal code bans speech and publications that threaten national security, insult Islam, or could "arouse people against the government," while other regulations make editors criminally responsible for the content of the material they publish. Officials are authorized to shut newspapers and sanction journalists for articles containing unfounded criticism of the government. Four writers for *Sandhaanu*, an Internet magazine, were arrested in early 2002; after being held in detention and charged with defamation, three were sentenced to life imprisonment and remain incarcerated. In this environment, some journalists practice self-censorship, although less than in the past. Today, newspapers are mildly critical of official policies (though not of specific leaders), and the state-run television station's news and public affairs programs discuss timely issues and criticize government performance. All broadcast media are owned and operated by the government or its sympathizers. Although the government owns the country's sole ISP, Internet access is generally not restricted. In March, the government amended the press law to allow for the closure of publications if they failed to publish regularly; it then cancelled the licenses of 22 such publications.

LEGAL ENVIRONMENT: 8
POLITICAL ENVIRONMENT: 10

Mali
ECONOMIC ENVIRONMENT: 9

Status: Free   TOTAL SCORE: 27

Mali's media are among Africa's most open. Freedom of speech and of the press is guaranteed in the constitution and is generally respected. Several laws provide for substantial penalties, including imprisonment, for libel and public injury, but they have never been used to prosecute journalists. However, in October, three reporters from a private radio station in Segou were imprisoned for several weeks after they were accused of criminal defamation. Equipment from the station was also temporarily confiscated in retaliation for their coverage of a local dispute. The state controls the only television station and a number of radio stations, but all present diverse views, including those critical of the government. At least 40 private newspapers operate freely, and more than 100 independent radio stations, including community stations transmitting in regional languages, broadcast throughout the country. Access to foreign radio and television transmissions and to the Internet is unrestricted.

Malta

Status: Free

LEGAL ENVIRONMENT: 2
POLITICAL ENVIRONMENT: 5
ECONOMIC ENVIRONMENT: 8
TOTAL SCORE: 15

As Malta is a member of the Council of Europe, media laws are based on European law. The 1996 Press Act protects freedom of the press, while the 1991 Broadcasting Act permits private commercial broadcasting. Following the enactment of the 1991 Act, broadcasting licenses were granted to the two major political parties and the Catholic Church, but other privately run radio stations and several TV channels have followed. However, many newspapers and broadcast outlets have strong political affiliations. A survey by the Broadcasting Authority showed that Maltese audiences perceive local television and radio news bulletins as politically biased, with excessive political content at the expense of nonpolitical local and international events. Three major weeklies and two dailies appear in both Maltese and English. Italian television and radio also reach Malta and are popular in the country. Locally, in addition to the public TV station, there are Super One TV, owned by the Malta Labor Party, and Net TV, owned by the Nationalist Party.

Marshall Islands

Status: Free

LEGAL ENVIRONMENT: 1
POLITICAL ENVIRONMENT: 5
ECONOMIC ENVIRONMENT: 6
TOTAL SCORE: 12

The government respects the rights of freedom of speech and press as provided for in the constitution. Sensitive political and cultural issues occasionally are handled with self-censorship by the media. A privately owned newspaper publishes articles in English and Marshallese. The government publishes a monthly containing official news but tends to avoid political coverage. Two radio stations, one government owned and one church owned, carry news broadcasts from overseas. The government station also provides legislative coverage. US military radio and TV broadcasts also reach some areas, and US television is available via cable.

Mauritania

Status: Not Free

LEGAL ENVIRONMENT: 23
POLITICAL ENVIRONMENT: 22
ECONOMIC ENVIRONMENT: 19
TOTAL SCORE: 64

In an uncertain political environment highlighted by an unsuccessful coup attempt in June and presidential elections held in November, Mauritanian media remained subject to considerable official pressure during 2003. A constitutional provision for freedom of expression is offset by a restrictive press law that forbids the publication or dissemination of reports deemed to "attack the principles of Islam or the credibility of the state, harm the general interest, or disturb public order and security." At least 10 independent newspapers were banned or seized during the year. Journalists are also sometimes subjected to harassment and arbitrary arrest at the hands of authorities. All publishers must register with the interior ministry and submit copies of newspapers to the ministry for review and possible prepublication censorship. As a result, private newspapers are unable to publish on a daily basis, and a number of journalists practice self-censorship. State-owned media outlets, including the only two daily newspapers and all broadcast media, slant coverage to support official policies. Although the government gave all candidates equal coverage on broadcast outlets during the November elections, opposition parties' access is otherwise extremely limited. However, foreign television broadcasts are available via satellite, and Internet service providers operate without government restrictions.

Mauritius

Status: Free

LEGAL ENVIRONMENT: 5
POLITICAL ENVIRONMENT: 10
ECONOMIC ENVIRONMENT: 11
TOTAL SCORE: 26

Press freedom is guaranteed in the constitution and is generally respected. Strict libel laws have not been used to inhibit the media. The Independent Broadcast Authority, established in 2001 and chaired by a government appointee, is mandated to regulate and license all radio and television broadcasting. A small number of private radio stations have been authorized to operate, but state-run media enjoy a monopoly in broadcasting local news and generally reflect official views. A number of private daily and weekly publications, however, are often highly critical of both government and opposition politicians and their policies. Several international broadcast news stations are available to the public by subscription.

Mexico

Status: Partly Free

LEGAL ENVIRONMENT: 11
POLITICAL ENVIRONMENT: 16
ECONOMIC ENVIRONMENT: 9
TOTAL SCORE: 36

After improvement in the earlier years of the Vincente Fox presidency, the situation of press freedom in Mexico remained somewhat stagnant in 2003. The Federal Law on Transparency and Access to Public Information passed in 2002, which was followed by an increase in access to government information, was a good first step, but its effect is still hampered by restrictions and the lack of any movement on the state and local levels. Many media outlets criticize the government openly, but journalists are occasionally sued for defamation. Libel is a criminal offense often punished with jail sentences. Reporters have been detained in Oaxaca and Chihuahua. The offense has even been charged in cases in which journalists had reported on government involvement in corruption and drug trafficking. In the state of Veracruz two journalists were attacked and another disappeared after reporting on connections between the state governor and regional drug cartels. Reporters from the Distrito Federal, Guerrero, and Yucatan states were ordered to appear in court to reveal sources. In Chihuahua the state government is said to have actively attempted to hinder reporting on sensitive cases. However, President Fox's decision to place crimes against journalists under federal jurisdiction has somewhat alleviated the culture of impunity that surrounded these crimes. Increased competition and the professionalization of the media have weakened the influence of government advertising, but concerns about loss of such revenue can still cause self-censorship. In various states government pressure on media content through the withholding of advertising funds has been reported. In Nayarit, the state government was accused of censoring a radio program and threatening to take away all advertising funding after opinions critical of the governor's administration were expressed on the program. The media generally operate in an open and transparent manner, and bribery of journalists continues to decline.

Micronesia

LEGAL ENVIRONMENT: 1
POLITICAL ENVIRONMENT: 7
ECONOMIC ENVIRONMENT: 11

Status: Free

TOTAL SCORE: 19

The constitution provides for freedom of speech and press. The national government and the four states publish newsletters. No daily newspaper exists, but two private newspapers are published weekly. Each state government also runs its own radio station, and one church radio station also broadcasts. Cable TV is available in three of the four states (Pohnpei, Chuuk and Kosrae), and Yap State has plans for a television receiver station. The Internet is playing an increasing information role; an estimated 1,700 inhabitants use it.

Moldova

LEGAL ENVIRONMENT: 22
POLITICAL ENVIRONMENT: 23
ECONOMIC ENVIRONMENT: 18

Status: Not Free

TOTAL SCORE: 63

Status change explanation: Moldova's rating changed from Partly Free to Not Free due to the enactment of restrictive new media laws.

Press freedom in Moldova deteriorated in 2003 as government authorities maintained tight control over national broadcast media while at the same time intensifying pressure on independent print media. Article 32 of the constitution guarantees freedom of expression and the press. However, existing legislation prohibits insults against the state and defamation of senior government officials. These provisions have allowed for a multitude of lawsuits against journalists in the dozen years since independence, and self-censorship is common. The new civil and criminal codes, which went into effect in January, contain still harsher penalties for libel, including prison sentences of up to five years. In March, a new Law on Combating Extremism was enacted, providing the government with another possible tool of media repression. The majority of print and broadcast media outlets are financed directly or indirectly by various political or ethnic interests. The state-run television station, Moldova 1, is the only station with national reach. Government efforts to strengthen the heretofore-nominal independence of the formerly state-run Teleradio Moldova, catalyzed by international and employee pressure, have not produced clear results. Since the beginning of 2003, direct and indirect pressure on Moldovan journalists has intensified. Transparency in media ownership is generally lacking, and Russian-language media receive a disproportionate share of advertising revenue vis-a-vis the Romanian-language press.

Monaco

LEGAL ENVIRONMENT: 3
POLITICAL ENVIRONMENT: 4
ECONOMIC ENVIRONMENT: 6

Status: Free

TOTAL SCORE: 13

The right to freedom of expression is legally guaranteed in Article 23 of Monaco's constitution, and the press operates freely. No press freedom violations were reported during 2003. The penal code prohibits insults of the monarch and royal family. No daily newspapers are published in Monaco, but French papers cover news from the country. There are two state weeklies: *Journal de Monaco* (published by the government) and *Monaco Hebdo*. The only television station is TV Monte-Carlo. Three radio stations cover the country: Radio Monte-Carlo Info, a French-language news and talk network; Radio Monte-Carlo, an Italian-language network; and Radio Monte-Carlo Moyen Orient, a pan-Arab station, now based in Paris and operated by Radio France Internationale.

LEGAL ENVIRONMENT: 11
POLITICAL ENVIRONMENT: 12

Mongolia
ECONOMIC ENVIRONMENT: 13

Status: Partly Free | TOTAL SCORE: 36

Despite some instances of official pressure, press freedom, provided for in the constitution, is generally respected. A 1999 media law bans the censorship of public information and also requires authorities to privatize all media. However, the government has delayed implementing this provision, and the majority of broadcast outlets, which serve as the main source of news for most Mongolians, remain under state control. Although political parties or business interests finance many private media outlets, both privately owned and state-run media continue to offer a range of views. At times the government files libel suits and launches tax audits against publications in the wake of critical articles. Libel charges are hard to defend against because the law places the burden on the defendant to prove the truth of the statement at issue. A court in 2002 sentenced the editor-in-chief of *Word* newspaper to one year in jail for libel, drawing widespread criticism from the media. In addition, lack of access to information continues to hamper investigative journalism and coverage of political issues. In this environment, some journalists practice self-censorship.

LEGAL ENVIRONMENT: 21
POLITICAL ENVIRONMENT: 23

Morocco
ECONOMIC ENVIRONMENT: 17

Status: Not Free | TOTAL SCORE: 61

Status change explanation: Morocco's rating fell from Partly Free to Not Free due to the enactment of new restrictive legislation and the increasingly authoritarian measures applied against the independent media.

Respect for press freedom in Morocco rapidly deteriorated in 2003. The passage of a controversial new antiterrorism law in May reversed many of the press freedoms only recently enforced by the revised 2002 press code. Since May, the government has invoked Article 41 of the antiterror legislation to suppress press freedom—setting stricter limits on and penalties for speech offenses—under the pretext of protecting Moroccan territorial integrity. Through subsidies, advertising allocation, and onerous regulation and licensing procedures, the government closely monitors and controls media content. The highly publicized case of Ali Lmrabet, the country's best-known satirist, sentenced to three years in prison on charges of insulting the king and undermining the monarchy, is symbolic of the recent crackdown on independent media. Although the flourishing of independent media in the late 1990s resulted in government tolerance of coverage of subjects once off-limits—the monarchy, Western Sahara, Islam, and corruption— these topics have become increasingly sensitive and a source of harassment and censorship for foreign and local journalists alike. As a result, self-censorship among journalists is commonplace. Though access to the Internet and satellite TV is generally unrestricted, the Moroccan government banned pan-Arab satellite TV station Al-Jazeera from broadcasting in the country in March. Broadcast media remain mostly government controlled. The authorities often exclude opposition views during election campaigns. However, there are plans to end the state monopoly on television and radio.

Mozambique

	LEGAL ENVIRONMENT: 13
	POLITICAL ENVIRONMENT: 17
	ECONOMIC ENVIRONMENT: 15
Status: Partly Free	TOTAL SCORE: 45

The 1990 constitution provides for freedom of the press but limits this right in relation to respect for the constitution, human dignity, the imperatives of foreign policy, and national defense. Criminal libel laws are sometimes used to prosecute media outlets for defamation; this poses an important deterrent to open expression and encourages self-censorship. In April, Supreme Court President Mario Mangaze sued the weekly newspaper *Zambeze* for libel over an article containing allegations of judicial corruption. The private media have enjoyed moderate growth, but publications in Maputo have little influence on the largely illiterate rural population. The state owns or influences all of the largest newspapers and also controls nearly all broadcast media. Although state-owned media have displayed greater editorial independence in recent years, the opposition receives inadequate coverage on national radio and television. The Higher Council of Social Communication, a press-law enforcement body, is dominated by the ruling party. Reporters continue to experience threats and intimidation, as well as a few instances of physical violence. In January, six men accused of the November 2000 contract murder of investigative journalist Carlos Cardoso were convicted and sentenced to lengthy prison terms. Investigators continue to examine whether the president's son, Nymphine Chissano, was involved in Cardoso's murder.

Namibia

Status: Partly Free

LEGAL ENVIRONMENT: 9
POLITICAL ENVIRONMENT: 12
ECONOMIC ENVIRONMENT: 13
TOTAL SCORE: 34

The constitution guarantees the rights to free speech and a free press, and Namibia is considered one of the more press-friendly countries in Africa. However, the government does sometimes restrict press freedom. In recent years, defamation lawsuits and other forms of legal action have been filed against several newspapers. Independent newspapers and radio and television stations criticize the government openly without explicit interference. Nevertheless, journalists at state-run media outlets have reportedly been subjected to indirect and direct pressure to avoid reporting on controversial topics, and they consequently practice self-censorship. In August of 2002, President Sam Nujoma appointed himself minister of information and broadcasting, prompting fears that he intended to assert further official control over the state-owned Namibian Broadcasting Corporation (NBC), which operates most television and radio services. One year later, the Media Institute of Southern Africa–Namibia continued to voice concerns about government reluctance to grant the NBC greater independence. Journalists are subject to verbal harassment and threats by government officials. The state's official advertising and purchasing bans on *The Namibian* remained in place as a result of the independent daily's critical coverage of President Nujoma and his government.

Nauru

Status: Free

LEGAL ENVIRONMENT: 2
POLITICAL ENVIRONMENT: 10
ECONOMIC ENVIRONMENT: 13
TOTAL SCORE: 25

Press and media are free; the government runs the only radio station. Nauru has no daily news publication, but three private bulletins are printed on a weekly or monthly basis. The radio station broadcasts

Radio Australia and BBC news reports. Nauru Television is also government-owned, but there is a private sports network. The government provides Internet service; because Nauru's telecommunications system is weak, service was unavailable for two months in January. Factional politics have resulted in parliament's replacing the president five times in the past year, prompting occasional, sporadic newsletters from opposition parties.

Nepal

Status: Not Free

LEGAL ENVIRONMENT: 20
POLITICAL ENVIRONMENT: 31
ECONOMIC ENVIRONMENT: 14
TOTAL SCORE: 65

Conditions for Nepalese journalists, which had deteriorated sharply as a Maoist insurgency escalated in late 2001, improved briefly with the signing of a ceasefire between the rebels and government forces in early 2003. However, when the agreement collapsed in August, the press was once again caught in the middle of the conflict and faced renewed intimidation and violence from both sides. Although emergency regulations were lifted in 2002, journalists (particularly those whom the government suspects of having Maoist sympathies) are still regularly arrested and detained, and a number have reportedly been subjected to harassment and torture. Media professionals are also under considerable pressure from the Maoists; suspected rebels killed a journalist with the state-owned news agency in September, and other reporters have been abducted and threatened or expelled from rebel-held areas. More than 200 journalists, defying a government ban on rallies, gathered in Kathmandu to protest the killing. Both the constitution and the Press and Publications Act broadly suppress speech and writing that could undermine the monarchy, national security, public order, or interethnic or intercaste relations. The government owns the major English-language and vernacular dailies; these news outlets generally provide pro-government coverage. While a plethora of private publications continues to cover sensitive issues such as the role of the monarchy, human rights violations, and corruption, self-censorship as a result of the intimidation detailed above is a growing concern. The government owns both the influential Radio Nepal, whose political coverage favors the ruling party, and one of several television stations. Private radio stations are required to broadcast Radio Nepal news at least once daily in addition to their own news programming. Access to cable television, foreign broadcasts, and the Internet is unrestricted.

Netherlands

LEGAL ENVIRONMENT: 2
POLITICAL ENVIRONMENT: 4
ECONOMIC ENVIRONMENT: 6

Status: Free

TOTAL SCORE: 12

The constitution provides for freedom of expression and the press. Although the relevant laws are rarely enforced, journalists can face imprisonment for insults against the monarch and the royal family. Commercial stations compete powerfully with public stations. Newspaper ownership is highly concentrated, as is that of commercial television, and many publishers also have interests in broadcasting; however, coverage remains vibrant, and there are no tabloids. In a remnant of the traditional pillar system, the state allocates public radio and television programming to political, religious, and social groups according to their membership size. Internet access is open and unrestricted.

New Zealand

LEGAL ENVIRONMENT: 1
POLITICAL ENVIRONMENT: 3
ECONOMIC ENVIRONMENT: 6

Status: Free

TOTAL SCORE: 10

The law provides for freedom of speech and press; according to the BBC, the country enjoys one of the world's most liberal media environments. Independent broadcasters compete with state-owned radio and television, and New Zealand's private newspapers and magazines cover politics tenaciously, offering a range of views. The Maori population struggles for more independent broadcasting and coverage; the government-subsidized Maori Television Service (MTS), scheduled to begin operations in June 2002, has been plagued with mismanagement and will not begin transmitting until at least March 2004. TV3 is appealing against a ruling made by the Broadcasting Standards Authority that an interview conducted with Prime Minister Helen Clark in July 2002, about allegations that the government had covered up a genetically engineered corn release, breached standards of balance, accuracy, and fairness.

Legal Environment: 10

Political Environment: 14

Nicaragua
Economic Environment: 13

Status: Partly Free
Total Score: 37

The press is slowly acquiring more freedom in Nicaragua under the government of President Enrique Bolanos. Press freedoms established under the constitution are widely upheld, although some seldom-used provisions exist that allow the government to censor the media for "accuracy." Privately owned print and broadcast media offer many political perspectives to the public, including criticisms of its current government. One disturbing trend, however, has developed in 2003: threats of serious violence were directed at reporters and editors of the national news daily, *La Prensa*, after it began investigating connections between drug traffickers and local police institutions along Nicaragua's Caribbean coast. A former Contra, Tito Moreno Aguilar, forced his way into the newsroom of *La Prensa* and took several reporters hostage after these stories began to run. He was later tried for the incident and ruled not guilty by a jury, in a trial marked by irregularities and evidence of corruption. Yet in a sign of the increasingly robust rule of law in Nicaragua, the Supreme Court overruled a decision by the treasury department to assess half a million dollars in back taxes against *La Prensa*, which had reported on alleged corruption at the agency under its former head, Arnoldo Aleman, who was also Nicaragua's president in late 1990s and whose supporters continue to exert wide political power in the country. No final decision has been made on an appeal to the Supreme Court on the alleged unconstitutionality of Law No. 372, which established an official Nicaraguan College of Journalists during the last year of Aleman's presidency.

Legal Environment: 20

Political Environment: 20

Niger
Economic Environment: 16

Status: Partly Free
Total Score: 56

Although the constitution guarantees rights to freedom of the press and of expression, the government continued to infringe on these rights in 2003. Libel and slander are regarded as criminal offenses and are punished by imprisonment as well as fines. In November, Maman Abou, director of the weekly *Le Republicain*, was tried in absentia and found guilty of defamation for an article alleging that the government awarded contracts to several businesses close to the prime minister without going through the competitive bidding process. His sentencing to six months in prison coupled with large fines triggered protests by the political opposition and civil society. The previous month, the publication director of the weekly *L'Enqueteur* had received a one-year suspended sentence and was banished from the capital for an article that authorities said incited ethnic hatred. Authorities also closed 15 independent radio stations during the year, but the move appeared to stem from a dispute over how licenses were issued rather than from a desire to limit press freedom. Other private stations were warned not to broadcast news that could "endanger peace and public order," according to the Committee to Protect Journalists. Coverage in the state-owned broadcast and print media reflects official priorities. Although a number of private publications freely criticize the government, journalists are regularly arrested and detained by police as a result of their reporting. Media outlets' financial viability is threatened by a law that imposes heavy taxes on private news outlets as well as by Niger's generally depressed economy.

Nigeria

Status: Partly Free

LEGAL ENVIRONMENT: 15
POLITICAL ENVIRONMENT: 23
ECONOMIC ENVIRONMENT: 15
TOTAL SCORE: 53

Freedom of speech, guaranteed in the constitution, is generally respected in practice. Although Nigeria possesses a vibrant and often critical media sector, journalists continue to face restrictive laws, physical threats, and economic pressures that sometimes curtail their ability to cover sensitive issues. Criminal defamation laws remain in place under which several journalists were detained, arrested, or sued during the year in connection with stories on state-level government officials. In February, the senate repealed three laws that critics claimed restricted press freedom. Freedom of Information legislation, which had languished in the previous house of representatives since 1999, was reintroduced to the newly elected house in June and passed its second reading. In July, criticism from media and civil society organizations caused the national assembly to withdraw a new code of conduct that required journalists to confirm all sensitive information from the assembly prior to publication and warned of punitive action in response to "speculative journalism." Nigeria has a vibrant privately owned media sector, including a number of publications and a handful of television and radio stations that are often critical of government. However, individuals outside major cities rely primarily on federal- or state-government–owned radio for information. They do often have access to international programs such as VOA and BBC services. No new private radio stations were licensed during the year. Both state and private media owners reportedly proscribe coverage of certain issues. Journalists, particularly those covering sensitive issues such as corruption, often run physical risks. Several journalists were assaulted or physically threatened during the year, including a photojournalist severely beaten on live television by police aides to the vice president. In June, state security officials claiming to act on orders of the president bought all copies of an issue of *Tell* magazine that alleged corruption related to All Africa Games contracts. Corruption is widespread in the media sector; many journalists and editors, though not all, accept payments to run or kill certain stories. While some media outlets discourage the practice, journalists report that the practice is actively encouraged at some others. Journalists are poorly, often sporadically paid and lack job security.

North Korea

Status: Not Free

LEGAL ENVIRONMENT: 30
POLITICAL ENVIRONMENT: 39
ECONOMIC ENVIRONMENT: 29
TOTAL SCORE: 98

North Korea's totalitarian government maintains strict control over all media and information. Although the constitution technically provides for freedom of speech, this right is severely restricted in practice. All media outlets are under direct state control, serve as propaganda outlets for the regime, and operate under strict rules of censorship. According to a report in the *Wall Street Journal*, ruler Kim Jong Il closely supervises the media, issuing monthly guidelines on acceptable topics for coverage and directing writers on how extensively they should criticize foreign governments. Citizens face a steady onslaught of pro-government news from radios and television sets that are pre-tuned to receive only domestic stations. Those caught listening to foreign broadcasts face imprisonment or death.

Ordinary North Koreans have neither the right nor the means to access the Internet. Very few foreign journalists are allowed into the country, and those who are able to report from North Korea are closely monitored and heavily restricted.

Norway

Status: Free

LEGAL ENVIRONMENT: 3
POLITICAL ENVIRONMENT: 3
ECONOMIC ENVIRONMENT: 3
TOTAL SCORE: 9

The constitution provides robust protections for freedom of the press. Truth is not an absolute defense in libel cases, and fines have been increasing. Censorship is illegal, but certain topics (such as suicide) are not considered acceptable material. Journalists abide by strict self-regulation, including the code of ethics of the Norwegian Press Association. Although Norway has the largest number of newspapers per capita in the world, just three large companies dominate the print media. The state provides newspapers with direct subsidies, which account for only 3 to 4 percent of their total revenue but serve to limit the impact of local monopolies.

Oman

Status: Not Free

LEGAL ENVIRONMENT: 26
POLITICAL ENVIRONMENT: 26
ECONOMIC ENVIRONMENT: 22
TOTAL SCORE: 74

Freedom of press remains restricted by the dominance of Oman's politics and society by its ruler Sultan Qaboos, now well into his fourth decade of rule, and 2003 did not see major openings for press freedom. Although the Basic Charter provides for freedom of press, government laws and actions tightly restrict this freedom in practice. Criticism of the sultan is prohibited by law. Oman's government permits private print publications, although many of these publications accept government subsidies. Journalists frequently practice self-censorship to avoid problems with government authorities. Despite recent demands from some members of the royal family to allow private television and radio stations, the government owns and controls all broadcast media, which have the widest reach with the Omani population. The government allowed state television to broadcast sessions in which members of the Consultative Council questioned government ministers. The number of Omani households with access to satellite television has increased, permitting a greater diversity of information sources, although this information chiefly concerns regional issues. Omanis can gain access to the Internet through the national telecommunications company, but the company blocks sites considered politically sensitive or pornographic.

Pakistan

Status: Partly Free

LEGAL ENVIRONMENT: 17
POLITICAL ENVIRONMENT: 24
ECONOMIC ENVIRONMENT: 18
TOTAL SCORE: 59

Pakistani media came under increased pressure from Pervez Musharraf's military regime during 2003. Although the constitution provides for freedom of expression and of the press, it and other laws authorize the government to curb freedom of speech on subjects including the constitution, the armed forces, the judiciary, and religion. Harsh blasphemy laws have also been used to suppress the media; in July, a sub-editor at the daily *Frontier Post* was convicted of blasphemy and sentenced to life in prison. Islamist groups and thugs hired by feudal landlords continue to harass journalists and attack newspaper offices; unidentified assailants killed Ameer Bux Brohi, a reporter for the Sindhi-language daily *Kawish* in October. On several occasions, police or security forces also subjected journalists to physical attacks or arbitrary arrest and detention. Foreign journalists experience visa and travel restrictions that can inhibit their scope of reporting; in December, two French journalists were arrested in Karachi and charged with violating these restrictions. While some Pakistani newspapers continue to be among the most outspoken in South Asia, many journalists practice self-censorship, and investigative reporting or direct criticism of the armed forces or judiciary is relatively rare. According to Human Rights Watch, which documented several cases of independent journalists' being pressured to resign from prominent publications or being arrested on charges of sedition and tortured while in custody, military authorities used increasingly aggressive tactics during the year to silence critical journalists. The Web site of an online newspaper established by editor Shaheen Sehbai, who remains in exile after fleeing Pakistan in 2002, has been periodically blocked by Pakistani telecommunications authorities since May. Although restrictions on the ownership of broadcast media were eased in late 2002 and media cross-ownership was allowed in July 2003, most electronic media are state owned and follow the government line. However, several new private TV channels available to cable subscribers provide live news coverage and a wide variety of political viewpoints. Authorities wield some economic influence over the media through the selective allocation of advertising, and both official and private interests reportedly pay for favorable press coverage.

Palau

Status: Free

LEGAL ENVIRONMENT: 1
POLITICAL ENVIRONMENT: 3
ECONOMIC ENVIRONMENT: 7
TOTAL SCORE: 11

The constitution provides for freedom of the press, and the government generally respects this right in practice. The media comprise three independent weekly newspapers, a government gazette, one government-owned and two private radio stations, and cable television. The Internet, though not used significantly, is accessible with no government intervention.

Panama

Status: Partly Free

LEGAL ENVIRONMENT: 19
POLITICAL ENVIRONMENT: 17
ECONOMIC ENVIRONMENT: 9
TOTAL SCORE: 45

Freedom of expression in Panama has been gradually eroded for decades. However, attacks on and legal prosecutions against the press have increased considerably in the last few years. Although prison sentences are generally commuted into fines, public officials frequently invoke repressive press and *desacato* (insult) laws to silence criticism, restrict circulation of information, and create an environment of intimidation and self-censorship among journalists. Indeed, over half the media work force have criminal libel or slander cases pending against them. Furthermore, with the judiciary subject to political manipulation and prosecutors' independence often compromised, Panamanian courts are not able to judge media cases independently. Although access-to-information legislation was passed in 2002, subsequent highly restrictive regulations rendered it worthless, and topics such as judicial corruption and government spending remain off limits. Although there is an abundance of independent and relatively diverse media, ownership of television and radio in particular is highly concentrated among former president Ernesto Perez Balladares and his friends and family. Direct economic barriers to establishing private media outlets are few, but the government exerts indirect control of the media through advertising distribution. Among other barriers to the independent media are government requirements that journalists and radio and television announcers must be licensed by the government and must hold a university degree in order to practice their profession.

Papua New Guinea

LEGAL ENVIRONMENT: 5
POLITICAL ENVIRONMENT: 11
ECONOMIC ENVIRONMENT: 9

Status: Free

TOTAL SCORE: 25

The constitution provides for freedom of speech and press, and media provide independent coverage, reporting on politically sensitive issues such as corruption. A law was proposed in April to prosecute anyone who publicly criticized the country or its government. In November Prime Minister Michael Somare, a former journalist, made further threats to press freedom, commenting that he was tired of reading media reports about official corruption. Transparency International rates the country as the world's 15th most corrupt nation. Independent newspaper, radio, and TV are present, in addition to government-controlled stations. Radio is an important medium due to low literacy levels and scattered settlements. In August, armed men entered the Bougainville offices of the *Papua New Guinea Post-Courier*, threatening to kill journalists Gorethy Kenneth and Eric Kone if further articles about the Solomon Islands' rebel leader, Harold Keke, were published.

LEGAL ENVIRONMENT: 15
POLITICAL ENVIRONMENT: 22

Paraguay
ECONOMIC ENVIRONMENT: 17
Status: Partly Free · TOTAL SCORE: 54

The Colorado Party has governed Paraguay for 56 years, including a 35-year dictatorship led by General Alfred Stroessner; Transparency International consistently ranks the country as the most corrupt in Latin America. Given such a political and economic environment, media ownership is highly concentrated and is heavily tied to the Colorado Party or business interests. Although the constitution provides for freedom of press and speech, investigative journalists often face considerable intimidation, especially when covering corruption or other criminal activity. Several reporters received death threats during the year. Legal pressures are also used to intimidate the press. Defamation and libel laws can be applied rather erratically and plaintiffs often receive a favorable ruling if they agree to share the settlement with the judge. Nonetheless, a diversity of views is present; most citizens rely on privately owned community radio stations. In 2001, the government repealed a restrictive transparency in government law, which sought to place hurdles to access to public information for investigative journalists, after it received severe domestic and international criticism. In its place, civil society organizations proposed a free access to public information law, which was debated in congress in early 2003. Press freedom advocates expect vague modifications that will further allow the government to hinder access to public information, such as Law 1628, which prohibits making public "sensitive" information about people and their assets, although the law does stipulate that it will not apply to journalistic work.

LEGAL ENVIRONMENT: 10
POLITICAL ENVIRONMENT: 14

Peru
ECONOMIC ENVIRONMENT: 10
Status: Partly Free · TOTAL SCORE: 34

The constitution calls for freedom of the press. In 2003, the recently enacted Law on Transparency and Access to Public Information provided for increased access to government information, including provisions preventing the classification of any information relating to human rights violations. However, a legislative decree passed during the year restricted journalists' ability to cover criminal trials. Libel is considered a criminal offense; libel charges are often used to harass journalists who work on cases dealing with corruption, especially those investigating connections between officials and drug traffickers. Cases of actual intimidation and violence against journalists decreased in 2003, but there were still occurrences in the provinces, including two that involved death threats to television reporters. Journalists were threatened for working on bribery cases and were also injured while covering anti-government protests. One paper claimed to have received threats after running a story about the private life of the president. Although outright attempts to control content are unusual, the knowledge that official pressure could fall on any group that produces negative stories has led to some self-censorship. Legal and financial pressure is also applied to intimidate media outlets. Media, which are predominantly privately owned, are diverse, representing a broad spectrum of political and social interests. For many rural regions, radio is still the most important source of news and information. The media corruption that was endemic under the Fujimori regime is still a problem. Some cases are still pending, while a number of media executives have been jailed on bribery charges; these convictions have led to a continued decline in trust in the media. It is also alleged that the Toledo government has played too large a role in the outcome of some of the legal proceedings concerning control of media outlets. Backlash from the corruption scandals has lowered the incidence of bribery among reporters.

Philippines

Status: Partly Free

LEGAL ENVIRONMENT: 6
POLITICAL ENVIRONMENT: 19
ECONOMIC ENVIRONMENT: 9
TOTAL SCORE: 34

Status change explanation: The Philippines' status changed from Free to Partly Free to reflect the continuing impunity enjoyed by those who threaten and kill journalists.

Freedom of the press, provided for in the constitution, is generally respected by the present government. Although Filipino media experience few legal restrictions, the editor-in-chief of an opposition newspaper was arrested on libel charges in August 2003. Most media are privately owned and reflect the political orientations of their owners, including powerful business interests or those with ties to political parties or officials. Nevertheless, the press is vibrant and outspoken, with a tendency toward innuendo and sensationalism. The greatest threat to the media remains the intimidation and violence directed at journalists, particularly those in the provinces. At least six journalists were murdered in 2003; most were killed after they criticized powerful local political leaders or reported on corruption issues. Other journalists received death threats, and media outlets were attacked during the year. According to the Center for Media Freedom and Responsibility in Manila, 17 journalists have been killed since 1998, and those responsible have not been identified or convicted, leading to a climate of impunity. In November, President Gloria Macapagal Arroyo announced that the government was offering a monetary reward for the capture of the killers of these journalists.

Poland

	LEGAL ENVIRONMENT: 6
	POLITICAL ENVIRONMENT: 6
	ECONOMIC ENVIRONMENT: 7
Status: Free	TOTAL SCORE: 19

Poland's 1997 constitution forbids censorship of the media. However, libel and slander are criminal offenses, and concerns over the chilling effect of lawsuits against journalists are growing. At the end of 2003, more than 40 investigations were pending against journalists and editors for violations of the press laws, defamation, or misuse of confidential information. In October, an international businessman implicated in a financial scandal in Poland's largest insurance company filed lawsuits against the publications that broke the story, and in November, a district court placed a gag order on the publications, barring them from running the story. Controversy continues over a 2002 broadcast law designed to limit cross-ownership of media by private companies, which critics claim was aimed at keeping the nation's main daily, *Gazeta Wyborcza*, from buying a stake in a television station. *Gazeta Wyborcza*'s editor-in-chief recorded conversations with film producer Lew Rywin, who allegedly solicited a $17.5 million bribe from the paper on behalf of the ruling Democratic Left Alliance (SLD) to amend the media rule in the paper's favor. The government appointed a parliamentary commission in February 2003 to look into the scandal, while Rywin's criminal trial for bribery began in

December. The concerns about concentration in media ownership that prompted the 2002 law have yet to be addressed. In a July article, *Newsweek Polska* wrote that media are subject to many forms of political and economic pressure from individuals and groups who may threaten a publication's financial security in retaliation for negative press coverage. The story stated that many publications may avoid sensitive topics for fear of reprisal.

Portugal

LEGAL ENVIRONMENT: 2
POLITICAL ENVIRONMENT: 5
ECONOMIC ENVIRONMENT: 7

Status: Free   TOTAL SCORE: 14

Freedom of the press is protected under the Portuguese constitution. Laws prohibiting insults against the government and the military are rarely enforced. Last year Portugal registered the largest increase in newspaper circulation in the European Union (EU), but it still has the smallest number of newspaper purchases among the EU member states. In addition to state broadcaster *Radiotelevisao Portuguesa (RTP)*, two private commercial channels operate in the country. There are two cable and one digital satellite operator. Of the more than 300 radio stations, only 7 transmit nationally. Use of the Internet is well below the EU average, with only 20 percent of the population regularly accessing it.

Qatar

LEGAL ENVIRONMENT: 14
POLITICAL ENVIRONMENT: 24
ECONOMIC ENVIRONMENT: 23

Status: Not Free   TOTAL SCORE: 61

Qatar took a small step forward in improving the legal environment for press freedom with the approval of a new constitution in 2003, but political and economic control remains in the hands of elites with close relationships with the royal family. The new constitution, approved in a referendum in April, offers guarantees for press freedom, and the state generally refrains from direct censorship. However, leading figures with ties to the royal family continue to influence content in print and broadcast media. Although the five leading daily newspapers are privately held, owners and board members of these newspapers include royal family members and other notables. As a consequence, direct criticism of the government is rare. A telephone call-in show sponsored by a government-owned radio station provided an opportunity for citizens to vent concerns about problems in public services. In March, the Emir of Qatar, Sheikh Hamad Ben Khalifah Al Thani, granted a pardon to a Jordanian journalist who had been convicted and sentenced to death for passing military and other information from Qatar to Jordan while working for the state-owned Qatar Television. Qatar is the base of the most popular satellite television channel in the region, *Al Jazeera*, which generally shies away from covering issues directly related to politics in Qatar.

Romania

LEGAL ENVIRONMENT: 13
POLITICAL ENVIRONMENT: 19
ECONOMIC ENVIRONMENT: 15

Status: Partly Free

TOTAL SCORE: 47

During 2003, Romanian media faced increased pressure and intimidation by authorities. Lawsuits against journalists and media outlets were quite frequent. More than 400 criminal cases were brought against the media during the year, the vast majority concerning defamation, which remains a criminal offense. Although prison terms for insult were abolished, they have been retained for libel or for "spreading false information." Most prosecutions resulted in excessive financial penalties or suspended prison sentences. The number of physical attacks on journalists who investigate corruption or other sensitive topics increased, especially in the provinces. In March, police found the body of Iosif Costinas, a journalist for the newspaper *Timisoara*, who disappeared in June 2002. Costinas had published articles on organized crime and was writing a book about illegal business activities in the area. Csondy Szoltan, a journalist for *Hargita Nepe*, was seriously injured by an unknown assailant, while Ino Ardelean, who works for the daily *Evenimentul Zilei* in Timisoara and frequently reported on illegal activities in the city, was beaten unconscious in December. He was the 14th journalist to be physically attacked in Romania in 2003. Media ties to government, business, or other powerful interest groups are still strong. The owners of private media are usually close to the ruling party, and public television is openly pro-government. Many privately owned media outlets suffer from a lack of editorial independence, usually serving the personal, political, and business interests of owners rather than advancing journalistic standards. Newspapers with the greatest editorial independence tend to be those that have some level of foreign ownership. There are 15 national daily newspapers, hundreds of local dailies, more than 70 private television stations, and more than 400 radio stations that are privately owned by Romanians. However, few Romanian media outlets are profitable. While the distribution system is state-owned and not always fully functional, advertising is sometimes used as a tool to pressure media outlets.

Russia

Status: Not Free

LEGAL ENVIRONMENT: 14
POLITICAL ENVIRONMENT: 30
ECONOMIC ENVIRONMENT: 23

TOTAL SCORE: 67

In 2003 press freedom continued to suffer as the Russian government exercised extensive control over most broadcast media and pressured the independent media. While the constitution provides for freedoms of speech and of the press, the Putin administration has increasingly restricted these rights in practice, especially regarding sensitive issues such as criticism of the president, the ongoing conflict in Chechnya, and government corruption. Using restrictive legislation and exerting financial pressure through the government and government-related companies, the Kremlin gained nearly total control of the broadcast media in 2003. Opposition political parties were denied equal and balanced coverage in the run-up to parliamentary elections in December. In January 2003, Boris Jordan, director of the largest private national television station, NTV, was sacked by officials from the media arm of the government-controlled gas monopoly, Gazprom. Many media analysts attributed the dismissal to NTV's critical coverage of the October 2002 Nord-Ost hostage crisis. In June, the remaining nationwide independent television station, TV Spektrum (TVS), was pulled off the air by the media ministry and replaced by a state-owned sports channel. The parliament passed media legislation in June that granted government authorities broad powers to shut down media outlets accused of printing or broadcasting "biased" political commentary during the elections. While the law was struck down by the Supreme Court in October, "many journalists had already turned to self-censorship, and editors curtailed coverage of the election campaigns to protect themselves from legal action," according to the Committee to Protect Journalists. The print media offered Russians some dissenting viewpoints, but the state-controlled and more widespread broadcast media parroted the government line. Independent journalists continue to be harassed, assaulted, kidnapped, and killed. High-profile cases of murdered or kidnapped journalists from previous years remain unresolved. In October, Aleksey Sidorov, editor-in-chief of the daily *Tolyattinskoye Obozreniye*, was stabbed to death, apparently in response to his paper's courageous investigative reporting on organized crime. The government severely restricted the ability of Russian and foreign journalists to conduct independent reporting on the war in Chechnya. During 2003, Russian government officials repeatedly pressured Estonian and Lithuanian authorities to shut down the Chechen rebel website KavkazCenter.com.

	LEGAL ENVIRONMENT: 24
	POLITICAL ENVIRONMENT: 33
# Rwanda	ECONOMIC ENVIRONMENT: 25
Status: Not Free	TOTAL SCORE: 82

Citing the contentious and provocative role of certain media outlets during the 1994 genocide, the present government sharply restricts the ability of the media to operate freely in spite of a constitutional guarantee of press freedom. In December, the International Criminal Tribunal of Rwanda convicted two journalists for their role in the genocide and sentenced them to life in prison. Despite a media bill passed in 2002 authorizing the licensing of private radio and TV stations, by year's end the government controlled all broadcast media. The number of independent newspapers is growing, but fearing official reprisals many journalists practice self-censorship, and coverage tends to follow the government line. During the campaign period leading up to national elections in August, the government used state-run media outlets to accuse the opposition of divisiveness and failed to provide equal media coverage for all the candidates as promised. Reporters continued to suffer intimidation, arbitrary arrest and detention, and deportation at the hands of authorities. In January, Ismael Mbonigaba, editor of the newspaper *Umuseso*, was detained for a month and accused of promoting divisiveness and discrimination. In November, *Umuseso*'s news editor, Robert Sebufirira, was detained and 4,000 copies of the newspaper confiscated after it carried an article investigating the demobilization of some army officers; five other *Umuseso* journalists were also briefly detained. Many independent newspapers are forced to print in Uganda due to the lack of printing presses in Rwanda.

Saint Kitts and Nevis

LEGAL ENVIRONMENT: 2
POLITICAL ENVIRONMENT: 9
ECONOMIC ENVIRONMENT: 10

Status: Free

TOTAL SCORE: 21

Press freedom is provided for in the constitution. The two main political parties, the St. Kitts–Nevis Trades and Labour Union and the opposition People's Action Movement, publish weekly newspapers. A third, non-partisan, newspaper also appears weekly. The government operates the only television station and the main radio station; seven independent radio stations also exist. Complaints from the opposition party center on accusations that the government limits or denies the party access to coverage on state-owned media; the party acknowledges that it has access to independent media outlets.

Saint Lucia

LEGAL ENVIRONMENT: 4
POLITICAL ENVIRONMENT: 3
ECONOMIC ENVIRONMENT: 4

Status: Free

TOTAL SCORE: 11

The country has traditionally enjoyed a high degree of press freedom; media are often critical of the government. However, a lengthy criminal code passed in November surprised and angered the island's media; the code contains a provision for punishment up to two years in jail for publishing false statements or news that could endanger the public interest. By year's end, no journalist had yet been convicted. The government partially funds a radio station and operates one television station. There are several independent newspapers, most of which publish on a weekly basis, two privately owned radio stations, and two television companies.

Saint Vincent and the Grenadines

Status: Free

LEGAL ENVIRONMENT: 1
POLITICAL ENVIRONMENT: 5
ECONOMIC ENVIRONMENT: 8
TOTAL SCORE: 14

The constitution guarantees a free press, and media openly criticize the government. There are several independent newspapers and radio stations, as well as a national radio station that receives funding from the government. The sole television station is privately owned. Some journalists complain that government advertising, an important source of revenue, is sometimes withheld from those publications more critical of the government. According the U.S. State Department, the government has recently adopted a policy aimed at distributing advertising revenue equally among the major newspapers.

Samoa

Status: Free

LEGAL ENVIRONMENT: 4
POLITICAL ENVIRONMENT: 8
ECONOMIC ENVIRONMENT: 12
TOTAL SCORE: 24

Samoa's press is generally free, though it is subject to some official harassment. Several English and Samoan newspapers appear regularly. According to the BBC, officials have sued the main private newspaper, the *Samoa Observer*, for stories on corruption and abuse within public offices. Officials have also cancelled government advertising in the paper. The government runs the sole television station, but additional stations from American Samoa are available. There are several radio stations.

San Marino

Status: Free

LEGAL ENVIRONMENT: 1
POLITICAL ENVIRONMENT: 7
ECONOMIC ENVIRONMENT: 6
TOTAL SCORE: 14

The Declaration on the Citizens' Rights and Fundamental Principles of San Marino Legal Order protects freedom of expression. The press operates freely; there were no reported violations of press freedom during 2003. A wide range of Italian media is available in San Marino. Two major national dailies circulate: *La Tribuna Sammarinese* and *San Marino Oggi*. The main broadcaster is San Marino RTV, a state-run TV and radio station. The only private radio station is Radio Titano.

Sao Tome and Principe

LEGAL ENVIRONMENT: 4
POLITICAL ENVIRONMENT: 10
ECONOMIC ENVIRONMENT: 14

Status: Free   TOTAL SCORE: 28

Freedom of the press is generally respected in law and in practice. There are six independent and two government-run newspapers. Three foreign radio programs are rebroadcast locally. While no law forbids the establishment and operation of independent media, the sole radio and television stations are government-run, with no privately owned stations. The law grants opposition parties airtime and access to the government-run media; parties freely produce and distribute newsletters that are critical of the government. In March 2003, former Prime Minister Pinto da Costa was convicted and given a one-month suspended sentence and fine for defamation and calumny for accusations made in an open letter to the National Assembly charging that President Fradique de Menezes had mismanaged funds and usurped government authority. Sao Tome's poor economic situation greatly restricts the growth and diversity of its media, as well as the ability of newspapers to publish regularly.

Saudi Arabia

LEGAL ENVIRONMENT: 29
POLITICAL ENVIRONMENT: 27
ECONOMIC ENVIRONMENT: 24

Status: Not Free   TOTAL SCORE: 80

Despite a general lack of press freedom, 2003 witnessed some measured increases in media independence in Saudi Arabia. Authorities do not permit criticism of Islam or the ruling family, and a national security law prohibits criticism of the government. This prohibition is echoed by a media policy statement, which also urges journalists to "uphold Islam, oppose atheism, promote Arab interests, and preserve cultural heritage." Official censorship is common, as is self-censorship. However, in 2003 newspapers reported on previously taboo issues—such as crime, corruption, women's rights, religion, and terrorism—without prior authorization. These instances of greater press freedom were largely catalyzed by the May 12 suicide bombings in Riyadh perpetrated by Islamist terrorists. The print media are privately owned but publicly subsidized, and the broadcast media are government-owned. Satellite television—through which Saudi citizens have access to foreign news channels such as Al-Jazeera and CNN—is widespread, despite its illegal status. Notably, the government banned Al-Jazeera from covering this year's Hajj and jammed the signal of the London-based reformist Al-Islah radio and television stations. The Internet is widely available but highly censored for content and monitored by authorities. Journalists must be licensed to practice their profession, and government authorities frequently ban or fire journalists and editors who publish articles deemed offensive to the country's powerful religious establishment or the ruling authorities. In May, Jamal Khasshogi, editor of the reformist newspaper *Al-Watan*, was dismissed on government orders for writing articles critical of the religious establishment. Two months later Hussein Shabakshi, a journalist who advocated for elections, human rights, and women's equality in one of his weekly columns in the Saudi daily *Okaz*, was banned from writing for the paper by the information ministry. In a positive development, in February the government permitted the creation of the Saudi Journalists Association, intended to represent the interests of media professionals. The government tightly controls the entry of foreign journalists through the granting of visas, though authorities were less rigid in 2003.

Senegal

LEGAL ENVIRONMENT: 12
POLITICAL ENVIRONMENT: 16
ECONOMIC ENVIRONMENT: 9

Status: Partly Free

TOTAL SCORE: 37

Despite constitutional provisions for freedom of expression and the press, observers expressed concern that the government of President Abdoulaye Wade increasingly felt the need to restrict these rights in 2003. Press laws that prohibit "discrediting the state" and disseminating "false news" are sometimes used to prosecute journalists. While the threat of legal penalties has resulted in some self-censorship, the independent print press and several dozen private radio stations are often highly critical of the government and political parties. Nevertheless, the only local television station is controlled by the state, and coverage favors the ruling party; in July, the High Audiovisual Commission, a media watchdog, criticized this station for not broadcasting news that might embarrass the government. Access to foreign publications and broadcasts and to the Internet is unrestricted. Reporters who cover sensitive topics sometimes face harassment at the hands of the authorities. Early in the year, several cases were reported of journalists' being assaulted by police as they attempted to cover the news. In August, Abdou Latif Coulibaly, director of the independent Sud FM radio station and the author of a book critical of President Wade, said he had been receiving anonymous death threats, which he blamed on members of the ruling party. Authorities expelled the correspondent for Radio France Internationale (RFI) in October after RFI aired an interview that the reporter conducted with a hardline member of the separatist Movement of the Democratic Forces of Casamance (MFDC). Senegal's interior ministry accused the reporter of trying to sabotage the peace process that is aimed at ending the two-decade-old conflict

Serbia and Montenegro

LEGAL ENVIRONMENT: 12
POLITICAL ENVIRONMENT: 16
ECONOMIC ENVIRONMENT: 12

Status: Partly Free

TOTAL SCORE: 40

While laws providing for press freedom are in effect in Serbia and Montenegro and in Kosovo, media independence was restricted in 2003 due to an unstable political environment, government pressure, and the threat of criminal libel suits. Following the March 12 assassination of Serbian premier Zoran Djindjic, the government imposed a 42-day state of emergency and significantly constrained press freedom. The publication, broadcast, or dissemination of information about the reasons for declaring the state of emergency and its implementation was prohibited, and several media outlets were fined or closed down (two permanently) for violating this decree. The government also enacted new and amended media legislation during the state of emergency: In March, the parliament passed amendments to the June 2002 Broadcasting Law, creating a Broadcast Council responsible for the distribution of national broadcast frequencies. Parliamentary attempts to appoint candidates to the council violated several provisions of the nomination process and led to the resignation of two council members. In April, the parliament adopted the Public Information Law, which addressed the rights and responsibilities of the media. According to the Committee to Protect Journalists, the law broadened "the ability of courts to close media outlets for using vaguely defined 'hate speech'" and weakened the protection of journalistic sources. The government also failed to fulfill its campaign promise of restructuring and granting greater independence to the public broadcaster, Radio Television Serbia. Libel remained a criminal offense, encouraging self-censorship. In Montenegro, despite new and improved media legislation, the government continued to exert excessive influence over independent media, and access to official information remained difficult. Journalists in both Serbia and Montenegro are subject to harassment, threats, and physical violence; no progress was made in solving the murder cases of journalists Milan Pantic (2002) and Slavko Curuvija (1999). In Kosovo, increased political friction exacerbated the harassment of and political pressure on the independent media. In response, Kosovar journalists have recently established the Association of Professional Journalists of Kosovo and the Association of Independent Media of Kosovo.

Seychelles

Status: Partly Free

LEGAL ENVIRONMENT: 17
POLITICAL ENVIRONMENT: 17
ECONOMIC ENVIRONMENT: 18
TOTAL SCORE: 52

The constitution provides for freedom of speech but also restricts this right by protecting the reputation, rights, and privacy of citizens, as well as the "interest of defense, public safety, public order, public morality, or public health." Civil libel lawsuits resulting in steep monetary penalties have been used repeatedly against independent media outlets. Sued for libel 10 times in the previous 7 years, the opposition weekly *Regar* was once again brought to court by the government in 2003. Although the private press continues to criticize the government, harsh legal penalties promote self-censorship. The state retains a near monopoly over the broadcast media, whose coverage adheres closely to official policy positions. High licensing fees have discouraged the development of privately owned broadcast media.

LEGAL ENVIRONMENT: 18
POLITICAL ENVIRONMENT: 20

Sierra Leone

ECONOMIC ENVIRONMENT: 20

Status: Partly Free

TOTAL SCORE: 58

Status change explanation: Sierra Leone's status improved from Not Free to Partly Free, reflecting a continued improvement in the ability of media outlets to report freely since the end of the civil conflict in January 2002.

Freedom of speech is guaranteed under the constitution, but the government sometimes restricts this right in practice. The 1965 Public Order Act makes libel a criminal offense not only for journalists and editors, but for newspaper vendors, printers, and publishers as well. In October, the government used this act to prosecute *For Di People* editor Paul Kamara and the owner and two employees of the printing press used to print the daily newspaper in response to an article criticizing the country's president. Earlier in the year, Kamara had completed a six-month prison sentence from a separate 2002 criminal libel conviction. In November police raided the offices of *For Di People* and confiscated equipment to pay civil damages awarded in connection with the 2002 case. The Independent Media Commission (IMC) is reportedly subject to government influence. The IMC did not suspend any private newspapers in 2003 as it had in 2002, and thus far has not followed through on threats to close radio stations that did not pay a high licensing fee instituted in 2002. Several dozen newspapers are published in the capital, including many that are privately owned and critical of the government. Radio, primarily state owned but with a growing number of private stations, is the most popularly accessible media source given the country's high illiteracy rate. Overall standards of journalism are low; media reports often reflect the political bias of the outlet's ownership. Corruption in the profession is reportedly endemic, with many journalists receiving payments to influence their coverage of issues.

LEGAL ENVIRONMENT: 23
POLITICAL ENVIRONMENT: 22
ECONOMIC ENVIRONMENT: 19
TOTAL SCORE: 64

Singapore

Status: Not Free

Media in Singapore remain tightly regulated by the government. The constitution provides for freedom of speech and expression but also permits restrictions on these rights. Legal constraints on the press include strict censorship laws; the Newspaper and Printing Presses Act, which allows authorities to restrict the circulation of any foreign periodical for news coverage that allegedly interferes in domestic politics; and the Internal Security Act (ISA). Although not used against the press in recent years, the ISA gives the government broadly defined powers to restrict publications that incite violence, arouse racial or religious tension, or threaten national interests, national security, or public order. The vast majority of print and broadcast media outlets, as well as Internet service providers and cable television services, are either owned or controlled by the state or by companies with close ties to the ruling party. For example, the government is legally mandated to approve the owners of key management shares in the privately held Singapore Press Holdings (SPH), which owns all general-circulation newspapers. Faced with the influence of owners over editorial content as well as the government's successful record of suing critics under harsh criminal defamation laws, journalists sometimes refrain from publishing stories about alleged government corruption and nepotism or the supposed compliance of the judiciary, or otherwise practice self-censorship. A number of independent Internet newsgroups provide a source of unfiltered news and opinion. However, the Committee to Protect Journalists reported that new regulations passed in November would empower authorities to monitor the Internet more aggressively. International newspapers and magazines are available, although authorities have at times banned or censored foreign publications that carried articles the government found offensive. The circulations of some Western-owned publications, such as the *Asian Wall Street Journal*, are "gazetted," or limited.

Slovakia

LEGAL ENVIRONMENT: 8
POLITICAL ENVIRONMENT: 7
ECONOMIC ENVIRONMENT: 6

Status: Free
TOTAL SCORE: 21

Media freedom is protected by the constitution, and numerous newspapers and magazines publish a wide range of political opinions and news articles. In September 2003, President Rudolph Shuster announced the decriminalization of defamation. Still, past defamation cases are proceeding, and a court ruled in October that the *Domino Forum* weekly was guilty of defaming former secret service director Ivan Lexa, who is suspected of involvement in kidnapping, murder, and other abuses while in power. The paper must pay him 1 million crowns ($28,500 US) for naming him the nation's "best known crook." Outside observers have also expressed concern that many television and radio stations are subject to political control because the membership of the councils that oversee them is comprised primarily of party and government officials. However, in December the parliament announced new broadcast regulations, effective in early 2004, that will place each station under the control of a three-member, government-appointed supervisory commission. The measure is aimed to curb corruption and mismanagement. In January, editors of the *SME* daily newspaper alleged that the government was tapping their phones. Tapes and transcripts of *SME* journalists' phone conversations were sent to political party officials, members of parliament, and rival media outlets over the course of the year. The newspaper has accused the Slovak Intelligence Service (SIS) of using illegal wiretaps to harass journalists and scuttle investigations into government and criminal misconduct.

Slovenia

LEGAL ENVIRONMENT: 3
POLITICAL ENVIRONMENT: 9
ECONOMIC ENVIRONMENT: 7

Status: Free
TOTAL SCORE: 19

Slovenian media are generally free to report on politics and other controversial issues. However, libel remains a criminal offense, and civil penalties may be levied against journalists who insult public officials. Self-censorship is sometimes practiced to avoid politically motivated lawsuits. On February 25, 2003, the National Assembly adopted the Law on the

Access to Information of Public Character to provide free public access to official information. The Journalists Association of Slovenia has since issued a number of protests on behalf of journalists who claim violations of the new law. Early in the year, officials made marked efforts to use the media to increase public support for a referendum on the nation's accession to NATO in March. Prior to the vote, the government spent the equivalent of its entire annual media budget to produce and place a series of broadcasts promoting the benefits of NATO membership. Officials also accused journalists who criticized the accession of "disregard for the national interest." Commercial pressure on many media companies to make a profit has reportedly trickled into the newsroom, leading to biased editorial policies and an increase in publication of advertorials, or paid advertising disguised as editorial content. The prosecutor's office continues to stonewall the investigation into the 2001 assault on reporter Miro Petek, who was investigating improprieties at a state-owned bank. Media concentration in Slovenia is considered to be the highest in Europe, with only six daily newspapers in the country. The Mass Media Act permits foreign ownership, but due to restrictions on ownership and cross-ownership, foreign capital has been slow to enter the market. Internet use is unrestricted, and about 40 percent of households are online.

Solomon Islands

LEGAL ENVIRONMENT: 4
POLITICAL ENVIRONMENT: 14
ECONOMIC ENVIRONMENT: 12

Status: Free

TOTAL SCORE: 30

Press freedom remains, and the media continue to report on controversial stories, including government misconduct, despite an economically ruined and politically hostile environment that led to an Australian military presence in the capital in July 2003. The country has been struggling to end fighting that broke out in 1998 between two ethnic groups on the islands of Guadacanal and Malaita. Militants occasionally threaten the media, and intimidation by government officials is common, but no harm to journalists was reported during the year. High illiteracy rates render radio broadcasting more influential than the print press. The Solomon Islands Broadcasting Corporation (SIBC), a statutory body placed directly under the prime minister's office, operates a public radio service that is the main source of information for most citizens. There is also a private

FM radio station and several independent weekly or semiweekly newspapers. No local TV service is present, although satellite television can be received.

Somalia

LEGAL ENVIRONMENT: 24
POLITICAL ENVIRONMENT: 33
ECONOMIC ENVIRONMENT: 23

Status: Not Free

TOTAL SCORE: 80

The Transitional Charter, as well as the constitutions of Somalia's autonomous regions, provides for press freedom, but this right is sharply restricted in practice, mainly because of continuing political instability and the inability of the Transitional National Government (TNG) to assert its authority over the country effectively. In 2002, the TNG enacted a new Press Law that requires all media to register with the minister of information and prescribes penalties for false reporting. Despite critics' concerns, there were no reports that the bill was enforced in 2003. The government launched its first radio station, Radio Mogadishu, in 2001, and private print and broadcast media have continued to proliferate. While some, such as the HornAfrik radio and television station, provide balanced and independent coverage, most outlets are linked to the various warlords and political factions. In May, regional authorities restored the broadcasting license of a company in Puntland; however, in September the Somaliland government banned all privately owned radio and television stations. Reporters continue to face harassment, arbitrary arrest, and detention in all regions of the country, and a number have been forced into exile. In January, armed militiamen allied to a prominent businessman attacked the HornAfrik radio and television station and temporarily shut down its broadcasts.

South Africa

LEGAL ENVIRONMENT: 7
POLITICAL ENVIRONMENT: 8
ECONOMIC ENVIRONMENT: 9

Status: Free

TOTAL SCORE: 24

Freedom of expression and the press, protected in the constitution, is generally respected. Nevertheless, several apartheid-era laws that remain in effect permit authorities to restrict the publication of information about the police, national defense forces, and other institutions, while the Criminal Procedure Act may be used to compel journalists to reveal sources. In 2003, a significant controversy emerged around the issuing of subpoenas to journalists by the Heffer Commission of Inquiry, set up by the government to investigate whether a high-ranking government official was an apartheid-era spy. National, regional, and international press freedom groups condemned the commission's ruling that journalist Ranjeni Munusamy, among others, would be forced to reveal confidential sources in court; however, the ruling was overturned in December. A variety of private newspapers and magazines are sharply critical of the government, political parties, and other societal actors. Radio broadcasting has been dramatically liberalized, with scores of small community radio stations now operating. The state-owned South African Broadcasting Corporation (SABC) is today far more independent than during apartheid but still suffers from self-censorship. Press freedom groups expressed concern that a proposed anti-terrorism bill posed a serious threat to democratic media. Reporters continue to be subjected to occasional instances of threats and harassment.

South Korea

LEGAL ENVIRONMENT: 8
POLITICAL ENVIRONMENT: 11
ECONOMIC ENVIRONMENT: 10

Status: Free

TOTAL SCORE: 29

Despite a change in government in 2003, freedoms of the press and of expression in South Korea continued to be generally respected, although provisions in the National Security Law are sometimes used to restrict the propagation of ideas that authorities consider Communist or pro–North Korean. In recent years, several journalists have been prosecuted under criminal libel laws for critical or aggressive reporting, and in August President Roh filed a civil defamation suit against four mainstream newspapers. Shortly after assuming office, Roh also replaced the press rooms at government departments with daily government briefings. According to the Committee to Protect Journalists, the move was criticized by larger media outlets on the basis that it limited their access to officials but was welcomed by smaller outlets that had been excluded under the previous system. Print media outlets, which are privately owned, scrutinize governmental policies and alleged official and corporate wrongdoing.

However, many are controlled by or associated with substantial business interests, and some journalists are also susceptible to bribery. Most broadcast media are state-subsidized but nevertheless offer diverse views.

Spain

Status: Free

LEGAL ENVIRONMENT: 3
POLITICAL ENVIRONMENT: 10
ECONOMIC ENVIRONMENT: 6
TOTAL SCORE: 19

The government's preoccupation with fighting terrorism led to an increase in the level of harassment that Spanish media faced in 2003. Ten Basque writers and journalists were arrested and three more held in continued detention under antiterrorist legislation. The Basque-language daily, *Euskaldunon Egunkariaa*, was shut down under suspicion of collaborating with the armed Basque separatist group ETA, and its editor was reportedly tortured while held for five days in prison. Al-Jazeera reporter Tayseer Alouni was arrested in August and remained in detention at year's end, allegedly for his connections with the terrorist group al-Qaeda. News media still wait for promised amendments to the civil code that would relieve them of the requirement to pay heavy fines in defamation cases. The magazine *El Siglo*, the online newspaper *Canoa-Diariodirectio*, and the TV station Telemadrid have all been hit by excessive fines for libel. The Spanish public broadcaster, Radio-Television Espanola (RTVE), operates two national television channels and four national radio networks. The two main commercial broadcasters are Telecinco and Antena 3. There is no official regulatory body for the press. Twenty newspapers account for about 70 percent of total circulation; 60 percent of all newspapers are owned by three Spanish media groups.

Sri Lanka

Status: Partly Free

LEGAL ENVIRONMENT: 15
POLITICAL ENVIRONMENT: 22
ECONOMIC ENVIRONMENT: 16
TOTAL SCORE: 53

Freedom of expression is provided for in the constitution. The government generally did not use legal restrictions on this right against the media during the year. However, the Liberation Tigers of Tamil Eelam (LTTE), a separatist rebel group, does not permit freedom of expression in the areas under its control and continues to intimidate and threaten a number of Tamil journalists and other critics. Reporters, particularly those who cover human rights issues or official misconduct, continued to face harassment and threats from the police, security forces, government officials, political activists, and the LTTE. In July, Fisheries Minister Mahinda Wijeskera threatened to kill Lasantha Wickrematunga, the editor of *The Sunday Leader*, after the newspaper published a series of articles accusing the minister of corruption. In several other instances, police or security forces manhandled reporters as they attempted to cover the news. While some journalists practice self-censorship, private newspapers and broadcasters scrutinize government policies and provide diverse views. The government controls the largest newspaper chain, two major television stations, and a radio station; political coverage in the state-owned media favors the ruling party. During the state of emergency declared in November, President Kumaratunga briefly deployed troops outside government-run media outlets, sacked the chairman of the government-owned Lake House media group, and replaced the editors of state-run print and broadcast outlets with her own supporters. Local and international observers expressed concern that the media were being used as a pawn in the political power struggle underway between the president and the prime minister. Business interests wield some control over content in the form of selective advertising and bribery.

Sudan

	LEGAL ENVIRONMENT: 27
	POLITICAL ENVIRONMENT: 33
	ECONOMIC ENVIRONMENT: 25
Status: Not Free	TOTAL SCORE: 85

The government continues to place severe restrictions on the ability of the media to operate freely despite constitutional provisions for freedom of expression. There are several daily newspapers and a wide variety of Arabic- and English-language publications. While all of these are subject to censorship, some do criticize the government. Domestic broadcast media are directly controlled by the government and are required to reflect official views, though some foreign programs are available. National security legislation empowers authorities to conduct prepublication censorship, confiscate or ban publications, and detain journalists. As a result, many journalists practice self-censorship. The quasi-official National Press Council is responsible for applying the press law and has the power to license and suspend newspapers. Despite a presidential decree in August promising to ease press restrictions, authorities continued to crack down on the media. In November, the *Khartoum Monitor*, Sudan's only English-language daily, was suspended for the seventh time in 2003 and remained shut down at year's end. The newspaper was charged with "crimes against the state" (among other allegations) for publishing articles addressing controversial issues such slavery, peace accord negotiations, and the independence of the Sudanese judiciary. Also in 2003, the government forcibly suspended a number of print media outlets, including *Alwan, Al-Azminah, Al-Ayyam, Al-Captain, Al-Sahafa, Al-Watan,* and *Raai al-Shaab,* as well as the Khartoum bureau of the Qatar-based television network Al-Jazeera. Sudanese authorities and security personnel routinely confiscate newspaper copies containing articles covering sensitive issues or deemed critical of the government. Under the penal code, propagating false news is punishable by either a prison term or a fine. Journalists are often subject to verbal and physical harassment by police and security forces, and some are detained without any specific charges. In November, *Khartoum Monitor* editor Nhial Bol fled to Kenya following repeated arrests and threats on his life, including a car accident that many in the press freedom community believed to be a deliberate attempt by the state to kill him.

	LEGAL ENVIRONMENT: 2
	POLITICAL ENVIRONMENT: 10
Suriname	ECONOMIC ENVIRONMENT: 6
Status: Free	TOTAL SCORE: 18

The constitution provides for freedom of speech and of the press, and President Ronald Venetiann's government generally respects these rights. However, some journalists continue to practice self-censorship due to a history of intimidation and threats under former dictator Desi Bouterse, who maintains his influence in politics. The media can face government warnings or harassing lawsuits from public officials when reporting on sensitive or critical stories; the U.S. State Department reported two such cases for 2003. The media are primarily privately owned, with approximately 11 private television stations and 25 private radio stations; state-owned broadcast media provide pluralistic views.

Swaziland

LEGAL ENVIRONMENT: 23
POLITICAL ENVIRONMENT: 28
ECONOMIC ENVIRONMENT: 26

Status: Not Free

TOTAL SCORE: 77

Freedom of expression is severely restricted, especially regarding political issues or matters concerning the royal family. Legislation bans the publication of any criticism of the monarchy, and journalists are occasionally prosecuted on criminal defamation charges. As a result, self-censorship is widely practiced. Journalists at Swaziland's only independent daily reported that they have trouble gaining access to official information. In August, MISA-Swaziland reported on government plans to impose stiff penalties on journalists found guilty of contravening a proposed secrecy act. The government controls almost all broadcast media and finances a daily newspaper, which both criticizes and defends government policies. On April 8, 2003, the new information minister, Abednego Ntshangase, announced that state-run broadcast media would not be permitted to "cover anything that has a negative bearing on government." This ban, which applies to Swaziland's only news-carrying radio channels and only television station, was condemned by the International Press Institute (IPI). However, broadcast and print media from South Africa are available. Reporters continue to experience some intimidation and physical harassment at the hands of police, security forces, and other societal actors. The government withholds advertising from the independent press and occasionally proscribes publications without providing adequate justification.

Sweden

LEGAL ENVIRONMENT: 2
POLITICAL ENVIRONMENT: 2
ECONOMIC ENVIRONMENT: 4

Status: Free

TOTAL SCORE: 8

Legal protections for press freedom, including freedom of information, were first established as part of the Freedom of the Press Act in 1766 and are enshrined in constitutional law. Newspapers are no longer closely connected with political parties, but their editorial pages continue to reflect their original affiliations. The state broadcaster dominates television, and media ownership is highly concentrated. Government subsidies provide as much as a quarter of the income of economically weak papers, although the subsidies represent just 3 percent of total press revenues. In April the media company Mediearkivet was ordered to pay 1,500 euros to a freelance journalist for illegally using two of his articles.

Switzerland

LEGAL ENVIRONMENT: 2
POLITICAL ENVIRONMENT: 2
ECONOMIC ENVIRONMENT: 5

Status: Free

TOTAL SCORE: 9

Switzerland remained one of the freest media environments in the world. During 2003 no violations of press freedom were reported. Articles 16 and 94 of the Swiss Federal Constitution provide the legal basis for freedom of expression and the press. However, the penal code prohibits racist or anti-Semitic speech. The largest-circulation daily newspapers are privately owned, chiefly by large media conglomerates. There is a diversity of smaller, regionally focused papers; however, they, too, are subject to increased media consolidation. The public Swiss Broadcasting Corporation (SRG SSR idee Suisse) dominates the radio and television sectors, but legislative efforts are currently underway to open these markets to more private competition. Due to market forces and the multilingual nature of the country, most private stations are limited to local and regional broadcasts. Internet access is open and unrestricted.

Syria

LEGAL ENVIRONMENT: 28
POLITICAL ENVIRONMENT: 32
ECONOMIC ENVIRONMENT: 20

Status: Not Free

TOTAL SCORE: 80

Syria's military-dominated regime continued to restrict press freedom severely in 2003; no significant changes took place during the year. Although the constitution provides for freedom of speech and the press, the overall legal framework for press freedom is weak, hampered by vague laws with clauses aimed at protecting the Baath Party's monopoly on power. The Emergency Law and the penal code ban publishing information that opposes the goals of the revolution and prevents authorities from executing their responsibilities. The Publications Law delineates the government's power to deny and rescind licenses for publications for reasons related to the public interest, which is not clearly defined. In July 2003, the Syrian government suspended the only independent weekly satirical newspaper, *Al-Domari*, for an alleged but unclear breach of the publications law. Except for a handful of radio stations that do not broadcast news, radio and television outlets are all state-owned. Citizens have access to the Internet only through state-owned servers, which block and censor content. Syrian security forces arrested Abdel Rahman Shagouri in February and held him in detention without trial for the remainder of the year, allegedly for distributing a newsletter from a banned Internet site.

Taiwan

Status: Free

LEGAL ENVIRONMENT: 9
POLITICAL ENVIRONMENT: 7
ECONOMIC ENVIRONMENT: 7
TOTAL SCORE: 23

The Taiwanese media remain among the freest in Asia. Constitutional provisions for press freedom are generally respected, and laws barring Taiwanese from advocating communism or formal independence from China as well as criminal defamation statues are not generally used to restrict journalists' coverage. However, continuing tensions with China contributed to official sensitivity about media coverage of national security issues and the military. In July, the high court sentenced journalist Hung Che-cheng to 18 months in prison for sedition over an article that allegedly revealed military secrets, although he was later granted a suspended sentence. Nevertheless, a wide range of privately owned newspapers reports aggressively on corruption and other sensitive issues; they carry outspoken editorials and opinion pieces. Government bodies, political parties, and the armed forces own shares in or are otherwise associated with the five main broadcast television stations and reportedly exert some influence over editorial policy and coverage. However, the widespread availability of cable television has diminished the significance of political party influence on broadcast television stations. In December, the parliament approved legislation banning civil servants or party officials from holding key positions in media organizations and requiring all political parties to divest themselves of ownership stakes within two years.

LEGAL ENVIRONMENT: 24
POLITICAL ENVIRONMENT: 27

Tajikistan

ECONOMIC ENVIRONMENT: 22

Status: Not Free   TOTAL SCORE: 73

Freedom of the press in Tajikistan did not register significant gains in 2003. While press freedom is guaranteed by the constitution and official censorship is banned, the government of President Imomali Rakhmonov suppressed the country's independent media through intimidation by tax authorities, the withholding of licenses, the denial of printing privileges by the state-run printing monopoly, the threat of criminal prosecution of libel, and strict secrecy concerning all government information. The government, which had for the first time allowed private radio broadcasts in 2002, denied the television broadcasting application made by Asia-Plus, the same media holding company that had initiated the country's first radio broadcast after the radio ban was lifted. The government cited a lack of technical equipment and qualified personnel as reasons for the decision, although Asia-Plus denied that the government had ever inspected the equipment or requested information regarding personnel. At the same time, President Rakhmonov continued to use the state-run media as a personal instrument of propaganda and harassed media outlets that published interviews or information about opposition parties. Tax authorities visited the independent weekly *Nerui Sukhan* and the Dushanbe prosecutor's office questioned its editor-in-chief following publication of an interview with an opposition leader.

LEGAL ENVIRONMENT: 18
POLITICAL ENVIRONMENT: 17

Tanzania

ECONOMIC ENVIRONMENT: 15

Status: Partly Free   TOTAL SCORE: 50

The government's efforts to combat terrorism and corruption have put additional strains on the right of Tanzanian journalists to impart information, a right enshrined in the constitution but routinely restricted in practice. Although the authorities do not officially censor the content of news products, the National Security Act, the Broadcasting Services Act, the Newspaper Registration Act, decency and criminal libel laws, and a "voluntary" code of ethics severely limit the media's ability to function effectively. The print media remain subject to strict gag orders, and journalists admit to self-censorship. As their numbers continue to grow, print and electronic media outlets have become more active, but their reach does not extend beyond the capital, Dar es Salam, and other urban centers. In this federal republic with large Muslim populations, the authorities on the semi-autonomous islands of Zanzibar maintain a separate set of media laws, which are generally harsher than national press-related legislation and are sometimes interpreted within the context of Islamic jurisprudence. In December, Zanzibar's leaders banned the islands' only private publication, *Dira*, revoked its editor's citizenship, and later banned a journalist from reporting for a 12-month period under the Zanzibar News Act. While there are no private broadcast operations on Zanzibar, privately owned radio stations on the mainland are not free to broadcast in tribal languages. They also remain under legal obligation to broadcast government-produced news programming every evening. Since 2001, when the government started a crackdown on the gossipy content of the tabloid press, journalists have been cutting down on their pursuit of scandals among the ruling elite, even though they are not convinced of the authorities' stated concern for the quality of local journalism.

Thailand

Status: Partly Free

LEGAL ENVIRONMENT: 12
POLITICAL ENVIRONMENT: 15
ECONOMIC ENVIRONMENT: 12

TOTAL SCORE: 39

Prime Minister Thaksin Shinawatra's government continued to exert pressure on the Thai media in 2003. Strong constitutional protections for freedom of expression are balanced by laws that enable the government to restrict this right in order to preserve national security, maintain public order, or prevent insults to the royal family or Buddhism. Though rarely used, the 1941 Printing Act gives authorities the power to shut down media outlets. In addition, libel charges were filed against several journalists and media advocates during the year. While the print media are largely privately run, the government and armed forces own or oversee most radio and broadcast television stations. Conflicts of interest remain a concern, as corporations controlled by Thaksin's family or with ties to the ruling party own or have shares in a growing number of private media outlets and exert influence over editorial policy. Despite an increasing level of self-censorship, some journalists continue to scrutinize official policies and report allegations of corruption and human rights abuses. Nevertheless, they faced a range of renewed economic and political pressures. Radio stations are required to transmit government-produced newscasts twice a day and must renew their licenses annually; media groups noted that renewals were sometimes delayed or withheld in order to punish critical stations. According to the Thai Journalists' Association, business associates of the government also withheld advertisements from news outlets in a further attempt to stifle critical coverage. Reporters were subjected to some harassment while covering the news, and a local journalist from the island of Phuket was murdered in February.

Togo

Status: Not Free

LEGAL ENVIRONMENT: 25
POLITICAL ENVIRONMENT: 32
ECONOMIC ENVIRONMENT: 21
TOTAL SCORE: 78

The September 2002 amendments to the 1998 Press and Communications Law further restricted press freedom by criminalizing defamation and requiring the licensing of journalists. These laws have since been regularly employed by authorities to harass and detain journalists and disrupt and close private radio stations and newspapers critical of the government. In early 2003, the High Authority for Audiovisual Communications (HAAC), Togo's official media regulatory body, temporarily closed private radio stations Nana FM and Tropik FM. Both stations had previously aired debates surrounding the legitimacy of President Gnassingbe Eyadema's intention to run for a third term in office. Further press intimidation occurred in late March when the communications ministry banned all foreign correspondents from reporting in the country. In June, authorities arrested three journalists at a cyber cafe and charged them with attempting to publish false information and disturbing public order as a result of their scanning photographs of persons who were allegedly physically abused by police and militia during the presidential elections. Despite government interference, an active independent press exists; more than 15 privately owned newspapers are known to publish opposition viewpoints and criticism of the government. A few private radio and television stations exist but tend generally to reinforce government policies. State-owned media outlets, including the only daily newspaper, the national television channel, and a number of radio stations, are dominated by pro-government agendas. The viability of many independent media is challenged by the reluctance of businesses to advertise with media outlets critical of the government. Intense financial pressures on journalists have left many open to bribery.

Tonga

Status: Partly Free

LEGAL ENVIRONMENT: 16
POLITICAL ENVIRONMENT: 17
ECONOMIC ENVIRONMENT: 11
TOTAL SCORE: 44

Although the constitution provides for freedom of speech and press, the government has pushed heavily this year to limit press freedom. The government attempted to ban the import and distribution of the independent *Taimi o' Tonga* newspaper several times in 2003, alleging that the paper aims to overthrow the government. The newspaper is owned by Kaliafi Moala, a Tongan with American citizenship, and is produced in New Zealand. In February, officials banned the newspaper after it reported on corruption allegations involving the government and royal family. After the Supreme Court ruled in May that prior bans directed toward the newspaper were unconstitutional, King Taufaahau Tupou IV in December signed constitutional amendments to tighten press laws that had been approved by the parliament in October. The Newspaper Act requires all publications in Tonga to be licensed by the government, while the Media Operators' Act restricts foreign ownership of media to 20 percent. Since then, the independent quarterly news magazine *Matangi Tonga* and *Kele'a*, a newspaper owned by a pro-democracy member of parliament, have also been denied licenses. In October, 6,000 people marched on the legislative assembly to protest against the constitutional changes that would limit media freedom and give more powers to the king. Protest marches are rare in this kingdom of 104,000 citizens; the last was in 1991. Despite the recent closures and denial of licenses, other public and private media continue to operate, though the state broadcast media practice self-censorship.

LEGAL ENVIRONMENT: 6
POLITICAL ENVIRONMENT: 10

Trinidad and Tobago

ECONOMIC ENVIRONMENT: 9

Status: Free

TOTAL SCORE: 25

The press is free; Trinidad has a vibrant mix of public and privately owned media, although many of the latter are owned by large business interests. Prime Minister Patrick Manning signed the Inter American Press Association's Declaration of Chapultepec in September 2002, joining other Latin American and Caribbean countries in defending 10 principles of press freedom. In signing the document, the government demonstrated a shift in view from Manning's predecessor, former Prime Minister Basdeo Panday, who refused to sign the agreement because of what he called the media's "dissemination of lies, half-truths, and innuendos." Rising crime, drug trafficking, and allegations of corruption within the police force are covered thoroughly in the press, resulting in some officials' criticizing the degree of "sensationalist" reporting. In 2003, the prime minister criticized the media's coverage of parliamentary proceedings as well as alleging that his own statements had been misreported; he threatened to initiate legal action against certain media outlets.

LEGAL ENVIRONMENT: 27
POLITICAL ENVIRONMENT: 30

Tunisia

ECONOMIC ENVIRONMENT: 23

Status: Not Free

TOTAL SCORE: 80

Since President Zine El Abidine Ben Ali seized power in 1987, the Tunisian media have been subject to repressive press laws, physical threats and arbitrary arrests, onerous licensing and publishing regulations, pervasive government control, and police surveillance. Despite a professed commitment to democracy, the government does not tolerate opposition and successfully stifles dissent through a system of direct and indirect financial, legal, and psychological controls. In response to continued harassment, fines, imprisonment, and suspension, media self-censorship is common. Although the constitution provides for an independent judiciary, the courts are highly politicized and influenced by the government. Moreover, the press code, with its broad, vague provisions prohibiting subversion and defamation, is frequently invoked to prosecute opposition voices. The government also restricts independent print media through its central censorship office and by controlling access to information, licensing and hiring of journalists, and the distribution of subsidies and advertising. In 2003 the government passed a law requiring all newspapers to increase the percentage of government-trained journalists on staff from 30 to 50 percent. A new election code was also passed prohibiting anyone from publicly discussing national politics on broadcast media during the two-week election campaign in early 2004. While Al Jazeera and some other foreign media outlets cannot operate in Tunisia, those that do are often subject to censorship. However, November 7 marked the establishment of the first private, albeit tame, radio station. The government did release award-winning Internet journalist Zouhair Yahyaoui from jail in November but maintained tight control over Internet accounts and Web site access. Although the government encourages journalist and student use of the Internet through 25-percent discounts, it also closed 80 public Internet cafes in 2003, reducing the number from 340 to 260. This year also included a significant campaign by press freedom organizations worldwide against the seemingly farcical decision to hold the 2005 World Summit on the Information Society in Tunis.

Turkey

Status: Partly Free

LEGAL ENVIRONMENT: 18
POLITICAL ENVIRONMENT: 23
ECONOMIC ENVIRONMENT: 11
TOTAL SCORE: 52

Constitutional provisions for freedom of the press and of expression are only partially upheld. In June 2003, the latest in a series of reform bills designed to facilitate Turkey's candidacy for entry into the European Union was passed; the new law formally permits previously outlawed Kurdish-language broadcasts on private stations and repeals a law banning "separatist propaganda" that had been used against journalists sympathetic to the Kurdish minority. A law on the right to access government information was published in October. However, numerous laws are regularly invoked to restrict freedom, including those against insulting state institutions such as the army, aiding illegal organizations, and commenting on ongoing trials. For example, Turkish generals filed a lawsuit against the Islamist daily *Vakit* and one of its columnists in October for an article describing the generals as pretentious and incompetent. Sinan Kara, a journalist known for articles criticizing local political leaders, was imprisoned in October for allegedly threatening the son of a former prime minister; Kara claims he was attacked by one of the man's bodyguards. Nevertheless, the number of journalists held in jail has dramatically declined in recent years, according to the Committee to Protect Journalists. A wide variety of independent print and broadcast media outlets provides a diverse spectrum of views. Most media outlets are owned by a few large holding companies that have outside business interests and in many cases refrain from excessive criticism of the government. In addition, broadcast media are regulated by the High Board of Radio and Television (RTUK), which temporarily closed at least 15 radio stations during 2003 and is reportedly subject to some political pressure.

Turkmenistan

Status: Not Free

LEGAL ENVIRONMENT: 30
POLITICAL ENVIRONMENT: 36
ECONOMIC ENVIRONMENT: 29

TOTAL SCORE: 95

Media outlets in Turkmenistan continued to operate in one of the world's most repressive environments in 2003. Freedom of the press declined from an already dismal state following the assassination attempt on President Saparmurat Niyazov in November 2002. The government flagrantly continued to disregard the guarantees of freedom of expression and access to information found in Turkmenistan's constitution. The government censors all sources of domestic media, controls all access to printing, and uses the mass media purely as a mechanism to promote the personality cult of President Niyazov and to attack his opponents. While all journalists working in Turkmenistan are under the constant threat of violence or prison for not toeing the government line, increased attempts were made in 2003 to crack down on Turkmen reporters working outside the country for foreign media outlets. Two separate incidents of attacks on Turkmen journalists working for Radio Liberty took place in Moscow in July and September. Another RFE/RL reporter was abducted, beaten, and threatened with death in November. Access to foreign news sources remains extremely limited, as does access to the Internet.

LEGAL ENVIRONMENT: 1
POLITICAL ENVIRONMENT: 6

Tuvalu
ECONOMIC ENVIRONMENT: 12

Status: Free TOTAL SCORE: 19

The constitution provides for freedom of speech and the press, but the media market is very small. The government publishes biweekly the only newspaper, *Tuvalu Echoes*. The single, government-owned, television station went off the air in 2001 for financial reasons but resumed sporadically in 2002. All copy to be aired on Radio Tuvalu, which is now run as a public corporation, must be approved by the Secretary to Government. He has reportedly occasionally blocked or delayed stories that are favorable to the political opposition. Many residents use satellite dishes to receive foreign programs, and Internet access is available.

LEGAL ENVIRONMENT: 16
POLITICAL ENVIRONMENT: 17

Uganda
ECONOMIC ENVIRONMENT: 11

Status: Partly Free TOTAL SCORE: 44

The basic law grants citizens the right to freedom of expression, but the authorities sometimes infringe on the ability of journalists to gather and disseminate information. In addition, the penal code, criminal libel and sedition laws, and the 2002 Anti-Terrorism Act criminalize "publication of false news" and other press offenses. There is at times an inordinate degree of self-censorship among journalists and news outlets covering an armed insurrection in the northern regions. This year, the government again banned radio stations in the northeastern town of Soroti from broadcasting any news about the rebel group known as the Lord's Resistance Army. In June, authorities charged the private Kyoga Veritaas FM of inciting panic and promoting the rebel agenda after it contradicted government statements that the rebels had abducted a number of civilians. The station was let back on the air on August 31, with some restrictions. Despite these enduring problems, the Ugandan media sector continues to grow and to improve in quality. Dozens of private publications and broadcasters now compete with the government's own media outlets, which include the popular daily *New Vision*; Radio Uganda, the only national radio station; and Uganda Television, which has been accused of strong government bias. The law still requires would-be journalists to possess university-level degrees, and newspapers can be shut down or denied state information. For example, in June, State House banned a prominent local columnist from attending presidential functions in retaliation for a story on the alleged crash of an Army helicopter in the rebel-held north in October 2002. Then in November, the attorney general prohibited the media from reporting on declarations of assets and liabilities by political leaders. As the nation awaits the Supreme Court's ruling on the legality of the law prohibiting the "publication of false news," journalists have been lobbying parliament to enact a freedom-of-information law, so far to little avail.

Ukraine

Status: Not Free

LEGAL ENVIRONMENT: 15
POLITICAL ENVIRONMENT: 29
ECONOMIC ENVIRONMENT: 24
TOTAL SCORE: 68

Media in Ukraine suffered at the hands of the administration of President Leonid Kuchma. Despite constitutional guarantees and the passage of new, nominally less restrictive media legislation, press freedom is significantly limited by libel lawsuits, license revocations, financial pressure, increased government control of the broadcast sector, and the physical harassment of journalists. As a result, many journalists practice self-censorship. In April, Kuchma signed a law clearly defining and prohibiting censorship, limiting financial rewards granted in defamation cases, and banning state and local governments from filing defamation lawsuits. However, these reforms are projected to have little effect on the practice of issuing regular instructions (*temniks*) to mass media outlets directing the nature, theme, and substance of news reporting. Many news outlets were reportedly subject to outright political control by the presidential administration. Libel ceased to be a criminal offense in 2001; instead, 46 civil libel suits were brought against journalists and media outlets in 2003. Criticisms of the government are most likely to be found in the print media, where high-circulation independent newspapers exist at the national and local levels. However, most major newspapers, financed by oligarchs pursuing their own political and economic interests, generally provide pro-government coverage. Government influence in the broadcast sector is almost absolute, as the state or pro-Kuchma interests control all six of the national television stations. The growing popularity of the Internet in Ukraine has led to a greater government effort to monitor web-based publications. In July, the government successfully filed suit to take control of the "ua" domain from a private firm and placed it under the auspices of the Security Service of Ukraine. Journalists are subject to physical assaults, death threats, and sometimes murder as a consequence of their work. According to the Institute of Mass Information, there were 42 assaults and threats against journalists in 2003. The case surrounding the 2000 murder of Internet journalist Georgy Gongadze continued to stir controversy, and in October authorities arrested former police officer Oleksander Pukach following allegations made by another suspect, Igor Goncharov, who died in police custody in August. Goncharov's allegations also implicated high government officials, including Kuchma, in Gongadze's murder. However, in December the Supreme Court granted Kuchma immunity from crimes committed while in office.

United Arab Emirates

LEGAL ENVIRONMENT: 27
POLITICAL ENVIRONMENT: 25
ECONOMIC ENVIRONMENT: 23

Status: Not Free

TOTAL SCORE: 75

The constitution provides for freedom of the press. However, the government restricts this right in practice. The law prohibits criticism of the government, ruling families, and friendly governments, as well as other statements that it considers threaten social stability, and violators are subject to imprisonment. Consequently, journalists commonly practice self-censorship; the leading private print media outlets frequently publish government statements without criticism or comment. While the main pan-Arab dailies are available and uncensored, other foreign newspapers, magazines, and periodicals are vetted by censors at the ministry of information and culture. The broadcast media are almost entirely state-owned and offer only official viewpoints. However, Dubai features a Free Media Zone, where few restrictions are imposed on print and broadcast media produced for foreign audiences. Satellite dishes are common, and international broadcasts are not explicitly censored. Internet access is widespread, although the authorities censor pornographic, radical Islamic, and antigovernment sites.

LEGAL ENVIRONMENT: 4
POLITICAL ENVIRONMENT: 8

United Kingdom

ECONOMIC ENVIRONMENT: 7

Status: Free

TOTAL SCORE: 19

The British government exerted undue pressure on the media during 2003. Media outlets were criticized for their coverage of the Iraq war, which was counter to the government position. The state-owned BBC's chairman of governors, director-general, and journalist Andrew Gilligan resigned in turn after the Hutton inquiry blamed the BBC for contributing to the apparent suicide of government scientist David Kelly, whom Gilligan had interviewed before reporting that the government had "sexed up" evidence to justify the invasion of Iraq. The survival of Britain's two most important conservative newspapers, the *Daily* and the *Sunday Telegraph*, is in question after the financial collapse of their owner, Lord Conrad Black. In October, the government approved commercial broadcasters Carlton and Granada to proceed with a £4-billion merger. The 2003 Communications Act eased media ownership restrictions and introduced a new regulatory body, the Office of Communications (OfCom), which will take over the functions of five previously separate regulators. Broadcasters were in favor of the new body, but print media were concerned that it might increase government interference with their activities. The old laws on copyright and confidentiality continue to pose a threat to the news media. Seven companies, four of which account for about 90 percent of sales, own the entire national press. The regional and local newspaper sector is also highly concentrated. There are four terrestrial television broadcasters, one of which is state-owned; cable is dominated by two companies. The state radio accounts for about half of all listeners.

LEGAL ENVIRONMENT: 3
POLITICAL ENVIRONMENT: 6

United States

ECONOMIC ENVIRONMENT: 4

Status: Free

TOTAL SCORE: 13

The major challenges to press freedom were issues related to coverage of the war in Iraq, the subsequent turmoil that accompanied coalition occupation of that country, and the ongoing war on terrorism. The press in the United States benefits from a legal environment that has consistently supported journalists in their pursuit of stories, limited the right of public officials to deny journalistic access to information, and narrowed the grounds on which officials can bring libel cases against the press. After September 11, 2001, the federal government increased the volume of classified information, and the Bush administration has been less open to contact with the press and less forthcoming with information than most recent administrations. Nevertheless, the press enjoyed considerable latitude in its coverage of the invasion of Iraq. Many press outlets chose to cover the war through the process of "embedding," in which reporters were assigned to travel with units of the invading forces. Embedding became a controversial policy, as a number of media critics charged that it led to the manipulation of the press by the government. On the other hand, some editors contended that embedding gave reporters unique access to combat zones. Editors were also pleased that the government did not impose formal censorship during the invasion. In the postwar period, the press has provided detailed coverage of the violent resistance to the occupation of Iraq and the often-rancorous debate within Iraq over the nature of the future government. The United States continued to draw criticism for measures taken in the wake of September 11, 2001. During 2003, the government refused entry to or deported a number of foreign journalists. In several cases, the government justified its action on the grounds that the journalists were functioning as intelligence agents. In other cases, the foreign reporters ran afoul of tightened visa guidelines instituted after 9/11. An ongoing issue for media freedom in the United States is the question of whether purchase of media entities, especially television networks, by large corporations limits journalistic freedom. In June, the Federal Communications Commission (FCC) issued a decision that would relax restrictions on the ability of newspapers to own broadcast media in the same geographical market. The decision triggered considerable controversy, with advocacy groups arguing that the new rules would contribute to an over-concentration of media ownership. The FCC rejected this contention, claiming that fears of media concentration are exaggerated in the age of the Internet and cable television. The new rules were under challenge in Congress at year's end, and suits have been filed in the federal courts to prevent their implementation.

LEGAL ENVIRONMENT: 7
POLITICAL ENVIRONMENT: 9
Uruguay
ECONOMIC ENVIRONMENT: 10
Status: Free
TOTAL SCORE: 26

The constitution of Uruguay provides for freedom of speech and the press; numerous private print and broadcast media outlets represent views across the entire political spectrum. The recently passed freedom of information act has permitted increased access to government information. However, libel, defamation, and contempt are considered criminal offenses; in March 2003 a journalist received a seven-month suspended sentence for libel. Laws against reporting "false news" and insult exist that carry sentences of up to two years in jail, but they were not used against the press in 2003. In September, a journalist reported receiving death threats as a result of his investigations into the links between police and an organized crime ring in the city of Paysandu. The tendency of state-controlled organizations to allocate advertising revenues only to pro-government media outlets has caused widespread self-censorship and even led to the firing of some reporters for articles deemed too critical of the government. Private companies have also scaled back on advertising, a development that has threatened the financial viability of independent media outlets already facing high distribution costs and an excessive tax burden.

LEGAL ENVIRONMENT: 25
POLITICAL ENVIRONMENT: 34
Uzbekistan
ECONOMIC ENVIRONMENT: 25
Status: Not Free
TOTAL SCORE: 84

The constitution of Uzbekistan both guarantees freedom of expression and information (Article 29) and, as of May 2002, bans official censorship (Article 67). Nonetheless, in practice press freedom is severely limited by the government of President Islam Karimov. The threat of conviction for defamation of the president, which remains illegal, and the continued physical harassment and intimidation of journalists leads to significant self-censorship on the part of editors and publishers despite the official ban on government censorship. In 2003 numerous cases of physical and legal harassment of editors and journalists were reported. However, the arrest, imprisonment, and alleged torture of Ruslan Sharipov, a journalist and the former head of the Independent Union of Journalists of Uzbekistan (IUJU), riveted the attention of international press freedom and human rights organizations. Sharipov, who had written numerous articles critical of the government, was arrested in May on allegations of sodomy, having sexual relations with minors, and managing prostitutes. Although Sharipov is an admitted homosexual and homosexuality is itself illegal in Uzbekistan, the fact that it is rarely prosecuted led most observers to see his arrest as politically motivated. Despite serious concerns about the reasons behind his arrest in May, the irregularities of his trial, and his claims of torture while in detention, Sharipov remained in prison in deteriorating health through the end of the year. Broadcast media remain subject to annual re-registration requirements, while print media remain heavily dependent on the state for both printing and distribution. In response to the government's lifting of the requirement for all Internet service providers to route connections through the state-run server, Uzpak, the availability of Internet access expanded in 2003, although Web sites considered objectionable by the government were frequently blocked.

Vanuatu

Status: Free

LEGAL ENVIRONMENT: 4
POLITICAL ENVIRONMENT: 8
ECONOMIC ENVIRONMENT: 11
TOTAL SCORE: 23

The constitution provides for press freedom. There is one government newspaper and a number that are privately owned. The sole radio and television stations are both owned by the state. The press is generally free to report criticisms of the government and its leaders without hindrance. However, the issue of media freedom was raised in September when a dispute between the Vanuatu Maritime Authority (VMA) and the *Daily Post* newspaper resulted in the newspaper's being served an injunction to stop reporting on the VMA or its staff. The VMA is under investigation for alleged mismanagement. In addition, *Daily Post* publisher Marc Neil-Jones was attacked by a group of unidentified assailants. Prime Minister Edward Natapei, approached by the Vanuatu Media Association in an appeal for press freedom, said he would resist pressure to curb the media.

Legal Environment: 22
Political Environment: 29

Venezuela

Economic Environment: 17

Status: Not Free

Total Score: 68

In the unstable political environment that has followed the failed coup against President Chavez's government in April of 2002, public and private media have turned against each other in a low-level civil war. Public media outlets support Chavez's policies uncritically and feed government-sponsored propaganda in coordinated television and radio broadcasts throughout the country. Meanwhile, private outlets have sacrificed their independence to support anti-Chavez factions. Consequently, the protections for independent media established by Venezuela's constitution are not enforced in practice; in fact, they are openly ignored by a judicial system firmly under Chavez's control. Journalists who criticize Chavez's actions are regularly prosecuted for defamation, slander, and contempt, all of which are classified as criminal offenses. In addition, journalists who provide the public with access to the opposition's views are routinely threatened with violence, attacked while attempting to cover the news, or otherwise harassed by authorities or government sympathizers. In October 2003, the government's telecommunications regulatory agency, CONATEL, confiscated live-broadcast equipment from a leading private Venezuelan news station, Globovision. President Chavez declared after the crackdown, "The permissive Chavez is over. We are and will continue to be vigilant as regards any excesses, especially by the news media, and we will apply the law whenever necessary." In cracking down against Globovision and other media outlets, the government abuses provisions in the country's Communications Law. Passed in 2000 after Chavez took power, the law stipulates that the government can move against media groups engaging in clandestine activities. Though no evidence exists that Globovision has been operating outside the law, the Venezuelan judiciary does not currently possess enough independent authority to review and override the government's crackdowns legitimately. A law of social responsibility in radio and television, which would nationalize all media and place them under strict ideological control, continues to be debated actively in Venezuela's national assembly. The current economic chaos in

Venezuela, spurred in part by Chavez's nationalization of major industries, makes private media dependent on the remaining major conglomerates for advertising revenue and economic survival. It also makes the major advertisers dependent on private media for their political survival, creating a corrupt reporting environment.

LEGAL ENVIRONMENT: 28
POLITICAL ENVIRONMENT: 30

Vietnam

ECONOMIC ENVIRONMENT: 24

Status: Not Free

TOTAL SCORE: 82

The Vietnamese media remain tightly controlled by the ruling Communist Party (CPV) and the government. Although the constitution guarantees freedoms of speech and of the press, both it and the criminal code contain broad national security and anti-defamation provisions that are used to restrict the media. In addition, a 1999 law requires journalists to pay damages to individuals or groups that are found to have been harmed by press articles, even if they are true. Officials have punished journalists who overstepped the bounds of permissible reporting by jailing or placing them under house arrest, taking away their press cards, or closing down their newspapers. All media outlets are owned or under the effective control of the CPV, government organs, or the army, and many journalists practice self-censorship. While journalists cannot cover sensitive political or economic matters or openly question the CPV's single-party rule, they are occasionally allowed to report on crime and official corruption. However, several of those that did so faced increasing threats and attacks from both government officials and private citizens in 2003, according to the Committee to Protect Journalists. Internet access is tightly restricted. Authorities block thousands of Web sites and require owners of domestic Web sites to submit their content to the government for approval. The regime tightened its control over Internet use in May by formally banning Vietnamese from receiving or distributing antigovernment e-mail messages and by setting up a special body to monitor Internet communications and prosecute violators. A number of cyber-dissidents were arrested or detained during the year, and several were sentenced to lengthy prison terms for their writings.

LEGAL ENVIRONMENT: 26
POLITICAL ENVIRONMENT: 22

Yemen

ECONOMIC ENVIRONMENT: 19

Status: Not Free   TOTAL SCORE: 67

The government continued to restrict press freedom in 2003 by tightly controlling its monopoly on domestic broadcast media, allowing vague laws restricting press freedom to remain in force, and intimidating journalists critical of government policy. Yemen's constitution provides for freedom of the press, but the overall legal framework regulating the press is weak. Article 103 of the Press and Publications Law prohibits direct personal criticism of the head of state, and the penal code provides for fines and imprisonment for publishing "false information" that "threatens public order or the public interest." The weakness of Yemen's judiciary and the ambiguity about who has the power to interpret the meaning of vague articles in laws affecting the press create an environment in which journalists do not feel secure in their right to criticize the government and debate issues freely. In 2003 the number of journalists detained and arrested declined, but reports of government intimidation of the media and of self-censorship among journalists continued. The ministry of information controls most of the printing presses in the country and provides subsidies to most newspapers. Only two newspapers own their own presses. The government enjoys a monopoly in the domestic broadcast media, which has a wider impact than the print media due to the high rates of illiteracy in Yemen, and it generally prevents reporting critical of the government in those media.

LEGAL ENVIRONMENT: 19
POLITICAL ENVIRONMENT: 24

Zambia

ECONOMIC ENVIRONMENT: 20

Status: Not Free   TOTAL SCORE: 63

Freedom of speech is constitutionally guaranteed, but the government often restricts this right. The Public Order Act, among other statutes, has at times been used to harass journalists. Zambian reporters and publications critical of the government are often charged under harsh criminal libel laws. In January 2003, three journalists from the independent biweekly *The Monitor* were arrested and another went into hiding after the paper published a story accusing the president's brother of corruption. Other journalists have received "warn and caution" admonitions from the government. The private media supported the introduction of freedom of information (FOI), broadcasting, and independent broadcasting authority draft legislation in 2002; however, the FOI bill was abruptly withdrawn after Vice President Enock Kavindele stated that it had "serious national security implications," according to the Media Institute of Southern Africa. The government currently dominates broadcasting, although an independent radio station, Radio Phoenix, presents nongovernmental views. This year, the private television station Omega TV was closed repeatedly by armed police officers, and the private radio station Radio Icengelo was threatened with closing after it served as a forum for opposition political parties. Coverage at state-owned media outlets is generally supportive of the government, and prepublication review at government-controlled newspapers means that journalists commonly practice self-censorship. Reporters continued to face threats and physical assault at the hands of police and ruling-party supporters.

Zimbabwe

Status: Not Free

LEGAL ENVIRONMENT: 30
POLITICAL ENVIRONMENT: 34
ECONOMIC ENVIRONMENT: 25

TOTAL SCORE: 89

Under President Robert Mugabe, freedom of the press continues to be severely limited. Authorities have broadly interpreted a range of restrictive legislation—including the Official Secrets Act, the Public Order and Security Act (POSA), and criminal defamation laws—in order to prosecute journalists. In addition, the 2002 Access to Information and Protection of Privacy Act (AIPPA) gives the information minister sweeping powers to decide who can work as a journalist in Zimbabwe and requires all journalists and media companies to register with the government-controlled Media and Information Commission (MIC). In September 2003, the Supreme Court ruled that the country's only independent daily, the *Daily News*, was not registered under the AIPPA and was thus illegal, prompting an armed takeover of the *Daily News* facilities in which the newspaper was closed down, its equipment confiscated, and up to 20 journalists detained. The government and police defied a subsequent high court ruling allowing the newspaper to resume publication, and the MIC refused to grant the *Daily News* a license under the AIPPA. Immediately following an October 2003 administrative court ruling that granted the newspaper the necessary license, police once again raided the *Daily News* offices, arresting 18 journalists and administrators. The government did not allow the *Daily News* to resume operations for the rest of the year. Section 15 of the POSA and Section 80 of the AIPPA criminalize the publication of "inaccurate" information, and both laws were used to arrest and harass journalists throughout 2003. This was in spite of the fact that, in a pyrrhic victory for press freedom, in May 2003 the Supreme Court had declared Section 80 of the AIPPA unconstitutional. There are no privately owned broadcast media outlets. State-controlled radio, television, and newspapers are all seen as mouthpieces of the government; they cover opposition activities only in a negative light. Independent media outlets and their staff are subjected to considerable verbal intimidation, physical attacks, arrest and detention, and financial pressure at the hands of the police, authorities, and supporters of the ruling party. Journalists are routinely barred from covering government activities or those of the opposition. Foreign correspondents based in the country, particularly those whose reporting has portrayed the regime in an unfavorable light, have been refused accreditation or threatened with lawsuits and deportation. In May 2003, Andrew Meldrum, an American correspondent for the United Kingdom–based *Guardian*, was declared a "prohibited immigrant" and ordered to leave Zimbabwe.

Freedom House Board of Trustees

About Freedom House

Founded in 1941 by Eleanor Roosevelt and others, Freedom House is the oldest nonprofit, nongovernmental organization in the United States dedicated to promoting and defending democracy and freedom worldwide. Freedom House supports the global expansion of freedom through its advocacy activities, monitoring, and in-depth research on the state of freedom and direct support of democratic reformers throughout the world.

Advocating Democracy and Human Rights: For over six decades, Freedom House has played an important role in identifying the key challenges to the global expansion of democracy, human rights, and freedom. Freedom House is committed to advocating a vigorous U.S. engagement in international affairs that promotes human rights and freedom around the world.

Monitoring Freedom: Despite significant recent gains for freedom, hundreds of millions of people around the world continue to endure dictatorship, repression, and the denial of basic rights. To shed light on the obstacles to liberty, Freedom House issues studies, surveys, and reports on the condition of global freedom. Our research is meant to illuminate the nature of democracy, identify its adversaries, and point the way for policies that strengthen and expand democratic freedoms. Freedom House projects are designed to support the framework of rights and freedoms guaranteed in the Universal Declaration of Human Rights.

Supporting Democratic Change: The attainment of freedom ultimately depends on the actions of courageous men and women who are committed to the transformation of their societies. But history has repeatedly demonstrated that outside support can play a critical role in the struggle for democratic rights. Freedom House is actively engaged in these struggles, both in countries where dictatorship holds sway and in those societies that are in transition from autocracy to democracy. Freedom House functions as a catalyst for freedom by working to strengthen civil society, promote open government, defend human rights, enhance justice, and facilitate the free flow of information and ideas.